Spirituality and Meditation

Order this book online at www.trafford.com/07-2217
or email orders@trafford.com

Most Trafford titles are also available at major online book retailers.

Note for Librarians: A cataloguing record for this book is available from Library and Archives Canada at www.collectionscanada.ca/amicus/index-e.html

ISBN: 978-1-4251-5094-5

We at Trafford believe that it is the responsibility of us all, as both individuals and corporations, to make choices that are environmentally and socially sound. You, in turn, are supporting this responsible conduct each time you purchase a Trafford book, or make use of our publishing services. To find out how you are helping, please visit www.trafford.com/responsiblepublishing.html

Our mission is to efficiently provide the world's finest, most comprehensive book publishing service, enabling every author to experience success. To find out how to publish your book, your way, and have it available worldwide, visit us online at www.trafford.com/10510

www.trafford.com

North America & international
toll-free: 1 888 232 4444 (USA & Canada)
phone: 250 383 6864 ♦ fax: 250 383 6804
email: info@trafford.com

The United Kingdom & Europe
phone: +44 (0)1865 722 113 ♦ local rate: 0845 230 9601
facsimile: +44 (0)1865 722 868 ♦ email: info.uk@trafford.com

10 9 8 7 6 5

Spirituality and Meditation

– The Quest for the Divine in Us –

Dan Barkye

To my wife, Sandi, with love.

- Be steady in the light -

Contents

Disclaimer

This book and its contents are for educational and informative purposes only, and only for such purposes.

The reader is urged to consult a medical doctor before practicing any advice from this book.

Acknowledgments

I wish to extend endless thanks to all who had faith in me and my project, the writing of this book—my family, friends, and most especially my wife, Sandi, who showed true limitless patience.

Many thanks to the Trafford company staff who helped me in the process of preparing the book for print and after that. Their gentle push to finish the book, was actually a big stick that prodded me to bring the writing to its hoped end. They are truly a font of help when needed.

Last but not least, many thanks to you, reader, for taking the time and the effort, no matter how little, to read this tome, and so to prove that its subject is of enough interest to justify it.

Some words before all others

Treading the way toward the Divine in me, I discovered a rich and wondrous world, far and deep inside and outside of my being, liberating and empowering.

From the beginning, the wish to impart to others this enriching experience was felt immediately and acutely, welling and gushing forth ever since. This proved to be a persistent need, which, in time, was transformed into a goal that I decided to pursue. This book is one of the results of this pursuit. Lecturing for a few years on the subject before the writing of this book, and advising others on these matters, were the other results.

I am trying, here, humbly, to show to anyone interested, the same bright lights that I discovered, lights that illuminate my life and the world around me with shining clarity that grows evermore.

By putting my knowledge and my thoughts on spirituality and meditation on paper, I present them in an organized manner, which, so is my hope, will elucidate some obscure and, in some cases, confusing corners.

The Divine resides in us and we are its temple. It does not tout its presence. It is silent and unassuming, but very much alert to every thought and action that it witnesses in our lives. Its silence is powerful, however, reverberating in our ears if we are willing to listen to its sublime sound, the sound of the divine eternal stillness and fixity.

It is our noble directive, so I believe, to acknowledge this presence in us, to search for it actively and, once it is found, to cling to it stubbornly and to try to listen to its voice, which is inspiring and transcendent. Following its echo in our soul may prove to be an unforgettable and helpful experience.

The road toward the Divine in us and toward attaining it and uniting with it, eventually, is demanding, but glorious; it enriches and enlarges the mind and the spirit, broadens and deepens them. This is the pursuit under which auspices the Quest for the Divine in us is taken.

When all is said and done, the Divine can be attained by anyone following the basic directive "Love your neighbor as you love yourself". Ultimately, this is all that is needed. Indeed, if one is content with following just this basic rule, all is very simple, but if the pilgrim engaged in this quest is interested to be more than just a basic, though diligent, pursuer of this goal, if he wishes to be more accomplished and skilled spiritually, then more than that is necessary.

If this is the case, a pursuit embedded in more complex spirituality notions is the best to tread. Upon embarking on this road, employing meditation would be most efficient, it being a most reliable aid.

The essence of this book and its message is just that, to delineate the spiritual way and to elaborate on it and on the tools that one who treads it would be wise to use.

The chapters dedicated to spirituality, the first two, are philosophical by nature, for we cannot touch on the transcendental without philosophising. In these two chapters, the basis for a spiritual life and conduct is presented. Besides a thorough exploration of the question of what is spirituality, they include principles that are immortal because they stem from the transcendental, which is the Divine.

The chapters inscribed to meditation are more practical.

Overall, though, philosophy and practicality are intertwined deeply in this subject, because spirituality is intended to be lived fully and, from a certain point of view, as much as possible while being connected to the world in which we live. And meditation, a practical tool, can easily lead to the spiritual, taking us to more rarefied levels of being and thinking.

If, however, the reader is interested more in meditation than in spirituality, then he may skip the first two chapters and go directly to the following four. The first chapter of this group, a very short one, is dedicated to the interaction and the integral connection between spirituality and meditation. In the second chapter, I expound an original explanation of meditation of what I perceive as a *Structured Process*. Furthermore, this explanation is the basis upon which the following two chapters that deal with other aspects of meditation are based.

The last chapter deals with the structure of the human body from the occult point of view and other pertaining matters, and with the benefits and drawbacks of meditation. They deserve proper attention.

The book abounds with explanations and information about issues and terms that are much used but never elaborated enough or at all for the person who is interested in more than the superficial and more than obscure instructions. Besides these explanations, the reader will find many novel approaches and notions regarding the subject matter.

I do hope that this depth dimension will be found valuable and will add to the experience, making the journey fulfilling and pleasant.

Chapter One

Those Heavens in Us – What is Spirituality?

...

The Quest for the Divine within

The man entered the room with a light and assured pace and, invited to do so, took a seat beside the presiding member. A crown of raven-black hair, lightly waved and well cut, adorned his head; a rather thick, neatly trimmed moustache and a warm, subdued smile, underlined the well-featured, tanned and symmetric face of a Caucasian complexion. His eyes, dark-brown, or were they black, it was hard to see, pierced the onlooker. He was young, in his early 30s, I guessed, and good-looking. One could tell he was a foreigner. Well dressed, though casual, exuding an emphatic self-confident aura, he had an imposing appearance.

The announcement stated that one of the most recent luminaries of the spiritual world of the '90s would come to us to give a lecture. *"Us"* was a local branch of the Theosophical Society. The theme of the lecture was *enlightenment,* and our visitor was the lecturer.

Well, enlightenment is something that everyone walking the path of spirituality is trying to attain. We were eager to hear what he had to say about it. Many of us, and I myself, had heard him earlier in other venues and his unique way of expressing his notions impressed us. Little did I know how profoundly and positively could a person be affected when walking The Way, the spiritual path, seriously and for a prolonged period. Among many other wonderful attributes, the spiritual experience bestows clarity of perception and great eloquence, and the man had them both. I know now that compared to him, many of us were mere novices at the time.

The meeting was thought provoking and quite strange, even for persons like me who were acquainted in some measure with the subject. Anyway, he looked at us intently for a few seconds, and then he posed to us a question. He did not start the lecture with a customary opening. He just threw his first sentence, this question, in the middle of the room for us to catch the rolling, surprising ball. And it was surprising. It was, however, a simple and straightforward question. He asked us the same question posed in the title of this chapter, "What is spirituality". It is an important question, it seems, if such an advanced person on the spiritual path presented it to us.

The question hit us right between the eyes. Well, we considered ourselves serious students of spirituality but, apparently, we never asked ourselves *this* question.

It surprised us that he presented to us such a query. Don't we know, don't we read about it daily, talk about it, discuss it ardently and try honestly to live by its precepts? We were sure that we knew the answer and even suggested a few versions. Oh, boy, were they not pathetic and pitiful, our tries? Our answers dealt, really, with what spirituality is *about*, not with *what* it is; they touched upon what one thinks about life from a spiritual point of view and how one ought to live spiritually. Apparently, none of us, really, gave the answer to "*what*" is spirituality, because, after a few attempts on our part, he gave up on us and offered the answer. He did it in a very original way. He approached the subject by stating what it is *not*!

Ironically, but making so much sense in a sudden instance of flashing understanding, he said, "Spirituality is not walking dreamy eyed among the flowers". Well, I must say that I agree with him. I agreed with it the moment I heard it. It was a revelatory insight, immediately and acutely felt. At the time, it was a novel revelation, and since then it serves me many times as a reminder for what spirituality really is. This definition of spirituality threw a new light on it from a very different perspective for me, the point of view of what it is not.

A lively and most interesting conversation followed. This is what we shall do now in this chapter.

The question that he posed has a much greater importance than meets the eye, for if we know the answer, we shall be able to achieve two objectives.

One, to answer the fundamental questions of our existence: What exactly are we, where do we come from, what is the purpose of our existence here in this world, and where do we go from here. These questions, doubtless, haunt humanity since its first inkling of self-consciousness.

The other, is the ability to choose, if we so wish, a course of action, according to the definition to which we arrive. Just as with any other goal in life, once defined, we shall be able to know if this is something that could and should be attained and then it is ours, or something bigger, more important, which offers some principles, in the light of which we shall choose a new way of living. Maybe it is something that, if adopted, will transform us in such a fundamental way that a new person will emerge out of the "old" us, a new individual, and maybe a better one.

It should be clear, intuitively, without even being spiritually inclined, that the question has something to do with concerns and issues that pertain to the contradiction between matter and spirit, and to the circumstantial of "the here and now".

As such, we look for something that, unlike matter, is not ephemeral, but stable and unchangeable. In other words, we look for something that is eternal, fixed and predictable, therefore utterly dependable. This "something" is self-sufficient, while matter is always dependant on external things, on some sort of external supply, to keep it in existence.

The answer to our question, therefore, is something that is imperishable and indestructible, literally. In short, it is a thing, which, *matter*, in every aspect, is not, no matter how we look at it. At this point, it can be stated without a doubt that spirituality is far beyond anything mundane that we may conceive as elevating above the material world in which we live.

To give a hint of what is to follow, the short description

above is what it is all about, the gist of it all.

Spirituality is one end of the spectrum of the human life's deepest essence and meaning, its other end being anchored in the dimensions of the physical world in which we live—matter, time and space. This definition, though, cannot be satisfying fully since it denotes a certain aspect of it, not itself as such.

Let us go on and try to find some more "negative" definitions of Spirituality, definitions that state what it is not. The parameters of this search will be qualities that demonstrate a refinement of the physical, material aspect of ours, something showing that we "see" beyond matter and aspire to what we perceive. This is what our visitor did. He looked into an aspect of our behavior that shows compassion, humbleness, love and affinity with our surroundings, but by the sheer comparison, he indirectly and subtly indicated that it is a poor, even ridiculous substitution for the true thing. Indeed, walking dreamy eyed among flowers, trying hard not to step on one of them, it being part of the Creation—whatever this may be for each of us— waiting for a butterfly to rest on our open palm, **is** love, **is** compassion and it **is** humbleness, indeed; however, it is not the answer. But before we finally embark on our inquiring journey, let us make an intriguing query: From the potential answers that will be posited here shortly, how shall we know which is the true one?

Natural Infinite Wisdom

To this question, the answer would be without doubt that we should know it immediately and naturally.

When contemplating a particular proposition or notion, it strikes a right cord in the deepest recesses of our being. When this cord is touched, it produces the right sound, the one that "says" in a definitive way "This is it, you have the right answer". It has the recognizable authenticity of the inner voice of the human being, a voice that does not need any external approval, the voice of the *absolute truth*. This voice exists in all of us. It stands solidly there, with a rock-stable presence, unshakeable and irrefutable.

When the truth is reflected in us, making its presence felt, we "hear" its sound, sensing it in a unique, distinctive way. It has the unmistakable seal of the truth that produced it, the signature that verifies and validates it. **This** is the voice of the Natural Infinite Wisdom in us, the capability to grasp and understand things with an ever present and alert, infinitely intelligent eye, without any need for initial or additional explanations, verbal or other.

"He who knows that he knows, knows!"

Upon hearing this voice, the next logical step is to make this knowledge a permanent and integral part of our personal bank of knowledge and of the perception of our existence, a part of our awareness.

This intuitive and empiric way of assessing the veracity of our assumptions on various notions will lead our way constantly when trying to understand and define such abstract ideas as the ones with which we deal now.

The Infinite Wisdom is something with which we are endowed from birth. This kind of wisdom is a perfect blend of intuition, empirical knowledge, mental faculties and an extended bank of knowledge. This knowledge bank is the transcendental, cosmic knowledge pool, a collective knowledge bank that includes all the information about everything that exists and occurs in the Cosmos, past, present and future, abstract—thoughts and notions, and concrete—actions and things.

This powerful tool is as natural to us as breathing. It was a prerequisite to survive when we came into this world at birth. In a matter of a split second, it assesses unknown things of every kind and nature and retrieves an answer that is fully acceptable and satisfactory to us.

We were born to live, so it makes sense that we were equipped with means to do just that – live, otherwise, Nature, Creation, would not bother. Since we were born naked, it makes sense that these tools are by definition an integral part of our organism, and that we can use them at our discretion.

For example, through a special physiological property of our skin, we, through our body, "know" how to defend ourselves against the countless number of bacteria that attack us every moment. We "know" how to "heal" a cut and a bleeding finger and make it healthy and whole anew. In the same manner, we "know" how to approach, assess and solve abstract notions.

For example, if we were not taught this, we would not know how to define a distance in yards or in other measure units. However, we could tell with almost absolute certainty that "the way to my home is so long from where I am that I will not make it in time for lunch", which can be much more than saying "the way is two miles long".

We said this because we heard the voice of the natural wisdom in us, an inborn faculty that offers an answer every time we need it, under any circumstances. Of course, experience and empirical knowledge have definitely their role in it, but in matters of transcendental nature, issues as God and Soul, even young children are known to have their glimpses of it, which means that for the analysis of such matters, experience and knowledge are not necessary.

All of the answers to **all** of the questions are within our reach, and always with us, because they are within us, they are a part of our structure, and so, readily accessible.

To emphasize the above statement, I would mention the well know phenomenon, the fact that many of the conventional science theories and discoveries were achieved while the scientist in question was in an "Intuitive Cognitive Mental Mode", if we may call this so. It will suffice to bring Archimedes' "Eureka!" and Newton's apple as the best-known examples of this state of mind, the intuitively cognizant one. In our times, *insulin* and *x-ray*, for example, were discovered through intuitive thinking that was disconnectd from the original theme on which the particular scientist was engaged at the time.

So, after presenting some thoughts on the possibility of verifying our findings, we are back on track to our subject, "What is spirituality". We shall try to find a plausible answer to this question and we shall take it from where the story ended.

Nature, Culture and Divine

I agree and endorse the notion fully: Spirituality, indeed, as the man said, is not walking among the flowers with dreamy, starry eyes, trying hard not to step on one of them, and with open hands, waiting for a butterfly to land on our palm.

Such a love for *Nature* is praiseworthy, for it shows compassion and empathy for the Creation. Having been endowed with ratio, we are the crown piece of it. As such, we have an initial responsibility from birth to nurture and preserve it and to recognize our position and behave accordingly. Still, this compassion and love for nature is not spirituality. True, it is an act of preservation of nature made out of unconditional love, not just to preserve it for future use, like the enjoyment of its sweet fragrance and lovely sight when coming again tomorrow to the sunny meadow, but it is not the answer for which we look. There must be a different definition, one to which our inner voice will respond more genuinely, and positively.

Let us look into another quarter of our life, one that shows this aspiration for the special kind of personal refinement mentioned earlier. Let us look into this infatuation of mind and heart with works of art of all kinds, let us consider *Culture.*

Well, it does not seem to be spirituality, either. Contemplating a painting masterpiece, reading an inspiring poem, watching a good play or a masterpiece of the seventh art, a movie, is not spirituality.

Even though all of the above, in part or in whole, is without doubt a wonderful and illuminating thing, none of it denotes the spiritually inclined person. Some, still "sleeping" people (we shall come to this descriptive term later), innocent and unsuspecting, may define it as such and actually do. However, when confronted with the definition of it, which follows suit, then, an open and receptive mind will immediately realize intuitively that all of the above is *culture* only. This is not to say that the culture that we humans developed is wrong or unnecessary, on the contrary, it is an unmistakable sign of our advancement but it is just not spirituality.

Culture, as refined and sophisticated as it might be, is but another aspect of **this** end of the spectrum of Creation, sunken deep in matter, the other end of which is spirituality. In spite of being of matter, culture is the result of the influence that this other, spiritual side of our being and of our inborn nature, exerts on us. We just want to lie back, occasionally, and do something that has nothing to do with eating and procreating and is as much as departed from it as possible. We yearn for doing something different from preparing the bed and the meals and from attending to our various needs in order to satisfy those instinctive necessities of our existence, something that elevates our spirit above this very existence and distances it from it.

Decorations are an integral part of not only humanity's leisure activity and pastime but of rituals as well, social and religious, and, from immemorial times, they involved some form or other of decoration and embellishment expressed in all forms of plastic art and music. It accompanies us in every aspect of our life. In birth and in death, in peace as in times of war, we try to make things more attracting and appealing to the eye, according to the circumstances and matching them. Why? Because we feel something, we hear an inner voice telling us to make things more agreeable to our more refined senses, different from the impending daily activities. It tells us to make something that awakens and starts the inner smile in us, heartening and taking us to a higher place, a place from which we can look upon it all and feel that we are not only the days and the nights, the work and the lunch break, the humans that we are, but something more.

This voice is the resonance of something higher in us, a higher level of being, the lower being the physical entity that we constitute. The *spiritual* in us whispers—it never shouts—but this murmur is loud enough to be felt distinctly, and so, by the very quality of its voice, to prod us into doing things that, from a materialistic point of view, are unproductive, like the occasional break from the daily chores or adorning them with a decorative touch. Strangely, though, we feel an enormous satisfaction when doing such things, and, equally strange, since we continue to do those "unproductive" things, this activity does not quench an ever-present thirst, a perpetual craving for another "place", another "feeling". These other places, other feelings, belong to a state of elation to a higher ground than the one upon which we stand, a station that has an eternal and stable nature as well, something that imparts a sense of endless presence.

No matter how masterly and matchless the cultural activities, this inner thirst is never completely satisfied. We are able to know this fundamental fact **only** when we perceive the bliss derived from attaining the spiritual in us, even if only momentarily. Yes, of course, when we attain it, we want it again, just as it happens when we are satisfied with a cultural activity, but the difference between the two is that the cultural satisfaction stems from matter and, as such, is ephemeral, while the other, the spiritual, is of a stable and permanent nature. The cultural satisfaction never really sinks to the core of our being. The spiritual satisfaction, on the other hand, which can be defined better as fulfillment, touches an inner cord that resounds with an unmistakable voice, "I am with you from the beginning of time and I shall be with you to the end of time". We know that this is true because, like all truly spiritual things, it stands by itself, self-justifiable, never in need to have the approval of an external, worldly authority. It is the maker, the product and the appraiser at the same time, all of whom, paradoxically, are detached from each other and objectively relative to each other. Compared to it, Culture is but a beautiful flower that, when autumn comes, withers. Spirituality is the evergreen tree that blossoms the year round.

Yet another, last possible place to find the answer to our question, is Spiritualism, or Spiritism.

This is the belief that we continue to exist after our death on another plane. Those who believe in Spiritualism are of the opinion that, after our demise, there is something that survives us. They define it "spirit", hence the name.

The leading concept, or belief of this movement, for it was very widespread by the end of the 19th century and still practiced today, is that the spirit of the deceased communicates with the living through various means. These communications are held, mainly, during what is called a "séance" session, but not only. Telepathy, clairvoyance, speaking during trance, automatic writing, dreams and more, are other means through which the spirit of a deceased person can be approached and, in turn, "speak" to us. This spirit, though, on which this movement is based on its assertions, is the astral body of the deceased, not its spiritual ego, these terms to be detailed later, in the last chapter. Therefore, in the search that we conduct, this is not what we look for.

The Quest for the Divine in Us

So if Spirituality is not Nature and not Culture nor Spiritualism, what, then, can that be?

Spirituality is the Quest for The Divine in Us

I would like to propose the following answer: The Divine in us is "The Self", the real, essential, immutable and eternal us, therefore the quest on which we are engaged is the quest for The Self, and this is how it will be treated, mostly, in this book, from now on.

This quest is, without exaggeration, the greatest adventure a person can undertake. There is a completely new world in us waiting to be discovered. Actually, we may safely say rediscovered and made significant to our awareness. When done in earnest, this can be a hard and demanding work, but it should not be discouraging, since it is a worthy and very rewarding endeavor.

Spirituality is the path that one engaged in the quest for the divine in him is treading, and the toil encountered. Many know it; they refer to it as "The Way". While on this way, the one undertaking this quest is known as "Walker" or "Seeker". I shall use the later term, mostly, throughout this book.

Once we make a step on this road, it is hard, if not impossible, to evade its impact, even when leaving it after a while. The imprint of its influence remains with us in our knowledge and consciousness forever, even when not influencing us directly, anymore.

A wondrous way it is. Looking back, the Seeker recognizes himself in every step he took, and by the end of it, when Self is attained, the Seeker morphs into The Way and both are The Self. When, at this point, the Seeker attains and grasps the object sought, the revelation presents itself, suddenly, that, by then, he is one and complete with it. Let us see how this happens.

The Metamorphosis

On this road, the Seekers are the active ones, looking for something that is there, is the real "Us", and is "waiting" for us to find it and reunite with it. At the end of the journey of active seeking and attempt of reunification with The Self, upon the fulfillment of these two goals, the Seeker is "it". We are this "something" which we sought; we are The Self. By then, we are a different person, one that had evolved immensely and in many ways. Moreover, this new person is an individual made complete, one who is reunited with his own Self.

The metamorphosis from a proactively aspiring entity—the Seeker, into a totally renewed one—the human being in us reunited and identified with his own Self, is a situation that deserves further explanation.

This is not a situation of finding something lost accidentally or something that we forgot where we placed it and, once it is found, put in the pocket. Not at all. This is a situation in which the realization dawns on us, finally, that, by the end of the journey, we, the seekers, underwent a process through which we were transformed into the very thing that we looked for—we found it, and, instantly upon finding it, identified ourselves, and reunited, with it. Let us talk about it yet a little more.

There are situations in which there arises an identification between the active and the passive participants of a pursuit and vice-versa. The interaction between them imparts to each one an imprint of the other; the mutual influence conveyed from one to the other results, eventually, in transforming each party into some sort of replica of the other, at least in some measure.

This is not the case here. In the quest for the Self, at the end of the day **we are** The Self, The Self being and remaining unchanged. Why so?

The cause for this amazing transformation is something that is an inherent part of our being. We have it, The Self, from birth. It is always with us, even though many of us, in fact, almost all of us, the overwhelming majority of humanity, are not aware of it. It is our unchangeable higher entity.

The reason for this profound change, the transformation of the seeker into the object searched, in this case The unchangeable Self, is that we are the place in which it resides. As a rule, we are oblivious to this part of our being in us.

This fundamental state of alienation is the result of the hypnotic sway that the surrounding physical world has on us. Because of its immediate impact, our attention is constantly diverted towards it—from within, outward.

We are thirsty, and, to the expense of anything else, we

savor in our imagination the pinching titillation of a sweet chilled soda in our mouth. We are cold and nothing else matters, only the miserable feeling that overwhelms us. We are hot, a mosquito bit us; we are insulted, we want money, we crave for titles, power, all of which are never of enough quantity and quality; we miss someone; we miss the physical proximity with our beloved, and, even then, we want more of it, endlessly more, and so on. All of this, perfectly natural things in the eyes of most of us, presenting itself in an ever–changing combination of items and quantity, is distracting us away from our inner world towards the world of matter around us.

However, let it be stated here and now, unambiguously: The inner world of ours is at least as rich as the outer, if not more. Treading The Way teaches us that it is richer, infinitely more so, and of a fundamentally different quality, superior and eternal.

The surrounding world exerts its influence directly on us from zero distance, point blank, enveloping us entirely.

Our skin is our last frontier

It defines the physical "us" in the world; it is our physical contour and it claims its needs in matters abstract and concrete, but even the abstract aspects of our existence, like love and honor, are only another facet of the physical man living in the physical world. Self has no part in all this. This is a fundamental supposition of spirituality.

The Self and its Source

The Self is an eternal abstract and immutable entity, unaffected by matter. It is the real "us", our authentic individual, identifiable entity, and driver. We are its temple of residence, carrying it through this world of matter in a fleeting journey, unbeknownst to most of us.

"We are in this world, but not of this world"

The Self is an integral part of The Universal Self, which

is its source and to whom it belongs. From its permanent place in eternity, where there is no time, no space, it is witnessing the fits and follies through which the physical human encasing it proceeds in his journey on earth, and absorbs them impartially, with an endless, unconditional patience, assimilating them for its evolution. The body is the carriage that The Self uses in its passage through the many progressive cycles of development that it is undergoing here, on the earthly plane.

The issue whether this is done through numerous reincarnation cycles, a widespread belief of the Eastern religions and philosophies but not only, or just a one-time appearance on earth, as many Spiritualists believe, is open to debate, and is unimportant in this stage. Now, all we have to know is that we are the home of The Self, and that The Self is in us, residing in its abode.

The Self and Us

The basic relationship between us, living physical human beings dwelling in matter, and The Self, is that we are like a suit for it, one that is changeable and fitted for the various cycles of its development, both on this plane, Earth, and on other planes of existence, a subject that will be touched upon shortly. However, taken as a whole, the relationship between The Self and us is ambiguous. We are disconnected from The Self and unaware of it and of the disconnection, from the very beginning of our conscious journey on earth. In this unapparent relationship, sometimes we suspect its presence with a very superficial and trivial, almost childish awareness. We can say and do things in the same breath that would contradict our own, shallow belief in The Self.

We identify ourselves unknowingly and unconditionally with our worldly existence, which, besides the physical body, includes a "body of feelings" and a "body of thoughts" (Please see Chapter Seven for an explanation of this subject). We are in an innocent state of self-identification with our physical body, not knowing anything else. Compared to the state of knowing about The Self and searching for it actively, this identification with the body and, through it, with matter, is but sleep.

When some insight, or some external means, remind us of The Self with a definite directness, then, an "awakening" occurs. Only when "awakened" we perceive that we have been "sleeping" and that we have been "sleeping" for the whole time before this "awakening".

For some, the "awakening" is a very strong and significant occurrence. From among them, experience teaches us that only some will choose to search for The Self actively. Of those, but a few continue to tread The Way for a lifetime in earnest.

Furthermore, we can compare the relationship between The Self and us to a wheel that is rotating perpetually, in which we are the wheel, The Self is the center of the wheel and the rotation of the wheel is the unfolding of our lives. Let us see how this comparison works.

When a wheel is rotating, the farther a point is on a wheel's spoke from the center, the faster it moves, to cover ground; a point on the rim rotates with the highest speed; the closer the point is to the center, the slower it moves. It follows from this that the center of the wheel, being an infinitely small point, is fixed, immobile.

Following this logic, The Self, being the center of the wheel in this analogy, is fixed and immobile, also. We, being the wheel, are not really rotating, of course, but moving in our life pursuits in the directions dictated by the circumstances involved. From its point in the center of this perpetually moving organism, which is us, The Self is observing our moves passively, while we are unaware of the whole situation.

Being oblivious of The Self on the existential conscious level, or, at best, suspecting vaguely its existence, we are in a perpetual state of disconnection and so, alienation, from it. This situation is further augmented by the social and technological developments visible all around now, developments that distance us from it even more, by emphasizing the human apparent ability to control its fate and course through the manipulation of matter to its advantage, through a defiant act of self-reliance. This is done by consciously and deliberately dismissing and excluding the possibility of any transcendental influence in our lives, influence which is named God by some, or Supreme Intelligence, Great Architect, or simply The Creator, by others, or Universal Self by many others, still. This noticeable development, most evident of late, is witnessed most strongly now by the transformation of the human society from a once moral into an immoral, and further, into an amoral one, especially in the West, spreading around the globe with an ever-increasing, frightening speed. All we have to do to glimpse this distressed, regretful state of affairs of ours, is to look around us.

It seems that the initial and perpetual state of disconnection and alienation from The Self is preordained. There could be a reason for it, besides what appears to be natural, and besides what we, as a human society, further do. This could be something that I suspect is a veiled and unperceived means of enabling us to make our way through this valley of tears. This possible reason could be as initial and preordained as the state that it enables, and just as natural.

The following assumption of mine is open to discussion, of course, and though, for the time being, at least, unlikely to be validated in any way, is worth mentioning and proposing, because it provides an interesting tentative explanation for this relationship between us and The Self. For what happens here?

The Self descends into matter repeatedly to develop itself through the experiences it will have through us on the Earthly plane of matter, as explained before. It does so by incarnating in a human being and draping its physical garment on itself. From a state of absolute abstract existence, purity and grace, from the extreme "spirit" end of the spectrum "matter-spirit", it "falls" into the other extreme end of this spectrum, the "matter" end, which is of the absolute density.

In this situation, if we, the home of The Self and as entities endowed with memory and ratio, had retained the awareness of the connection with The Self in our earthly ego, the journey here, on Earth, would have been impossible.

It would have been unbearable for the human part of our being to know that this place, here, is not our real home but only a class-room, and what we do in it is being subjected to trials and to lessons to be drawn from them. Able to confront this knowledge with the fact that we are here only temporarily and with a retained memory of the blissful place that is the source of The Self, would have caused a lifetime of suffering and deep, continuous frustration, besides the ones entailed by an existence entrapped in matter.

Imagine yourself hiking in the forest, climbing up and down mountains and valleys, sweating, hungry and thirsty, and so tired, sometimes, that you wish you would have never taken this trip with all its trouble and that it would all end then and there. You wish you were sitting comfortably in your soft living-room chair, sipping a cool drink, listening to a lovable tune, chatting with your friend about this and that, not caring about anything at all. However, you cannot do this, so you try to forget for the time being about home and its comfort, and go on dragging your sorry bones through the bushes and the stones, the rocks and the thorns. If you keep thinking about it all the time and bemoaning it, it will only upset and weaken you. You know this, so you try with all your might to remove it from your mind. Most of the time you succeed, and, anyway, the hike has its nice and pleasant moments, but the hardships and the disappointments, the sufferings, are there with you always.

If the memory of our real source had been with us in the journey we are undertaking on behalf of our inhabitant, The Self, this is how we would feel.

I remember a science-fiction story about the preparations that the pilots of an inter-galactic space-ships fleet undertook to overcome the hardships of homesickness and isolation that they would encounter in their long flights.

Shortly before taking off from home to their final destination, they would go through a psychological treatment, brainwashing themselves to despise home and family, wishing to be as far as possible from them. Before coming back, they would go through an inverse treatment, reverting themselves to a state of missing home deeply in order to make the hardships of the long trip home worthwhile and bearable.

Likewise, the assumption of a preordained disconnection between The Self and us implies that the cosmic mechanism of the reincarnation of Self imposes on its home, the human being, a state of forgetfulness about his real source and identity and his task in this affair, making this journey through matter endurable and tolerable.

Now, the legitimate question to ask would be "If so, then why bother to reconnect with my Self? Only to increase my sorrow?" The answer to this fair question, unrelated to my assumption, but applicable, nevertheless, is that it is advised that such a quest be contemplated and undertaken only late in life, when one has already fulfilled the need to satisfy the worldly temptations in their greater part. Confucius, the great Chinese sage, said that this journey is to be taken at the age of forty; remember that in those times, people lived shorter, so the current equivalent for this age would be about fifty at least. Regarding this same matter, the Hindu religion states that only when one had attended fully to his house and had seen his own children in the midst of their own families, can he leave his home, go into the world and become a monk, an undertaking that is supposed to bring one nearer to The Self.

Given the two explanations for the disconnection between The Self and us, the, tentative, cosmic reason, and the inherent human sociological and technological developments that widens it further, we can understand better, now, the relationship between it and us.

One explanation, mine, implies a manipulation done on us in order to be able to sustain the hardships of the life we live on earth on behalf of the dweller in us, to which we serve as its temple. This manipulation is assisted by the hypnosis that matter exercises on us.

The other explanation, the inherent human state of being, states that this hypothetical assistance took a life of its own and is predisposing us to deny our true heritage consciously and deliberately, even when glimpsing its rays, and to perceive matter as all there is. This is pursued in a stubborn and defiant persistence to rely on ourselves, while distancing from the transcendental and the eternal more than necessary from the first explanation.

In this state of alienation on our part towards it, The Self, in its fixity and immobility, is witnessing our humanly existence on Earth, absorbing and assimilating it in an absolutely impartial and non-judgmental manner.

Ever growing in knowledge through our life experiences in their entirety, without paying attention to good or bad, right or wrong, correct or incorrect, The Self is developing through the cycles of life through which we march in the process of reincarnation, which, so I believe, is our law of existence.

The Journey of The Self

The personal Self started its individualized journey by parting itself as a tiny bit, a "spark" in the occult parlance, from the Universal Self. The partition of the individual Self from the Universal Self happened purposefully and willingly.

The reason for this division is the desire of the Universal Self to learn about existence—which is a direct result of The Creation, Its own making—in all its forms and complexities. To attain this goal, It has to "live" on all the various, consecutive planes of existence, from the physical plane at first, to the most elevated one, below Itself, in this order. It does so by letting off innumerable tiny particles that start their descent into matter and ascend back again, upward, to their source, devolving and evolving in the process. When this tiny particle, the Individual Self, reaches the plane of the Universal Self after completing the journey back and forth through all the planes, it merges with It, and so, is one with It again. Enriched by the experiences it had on all the planes of existence throughout the life cycles of the human beings in which it incarnated, it enriches the Universal Self in Its turn, thus fulfilling its initial mission.

The human life as perceived by the occult, is arranged around a *seed of existence*, which is the *spark* mentioned, that "incarnates" in a human body. From that initial instance of incarnation, it then repeats it, "incarnating" anew in different bodies in different times, places and circumstances, according to a predetermined plan conceived by this individual original seed every time before it starts a new incarnation cycle, therefore the re*incarnation* term found in so many narrations on the subject. Some Eastern schools propound incarnation in animal bodies also, perceived, of course, as a lower state of being, beneath human. I do not subscribe to this doctrine because the evolvement of the human is an unchangeable upward advancement, toward his creator, not backward, even if temporarily.

This repetitive cycle of incarnation is bound to end when its purpose has been achieved.

Let us spend a few words here about this doctrine, to shed light on the circumstances that cause this cosmic activity—the place from which the seeds emerge and the reason that they do it.

One explanation as for **why** this happens is found in the Kabbalah. It even has a name for it, "Bread of Disgrace". According to this account, these seeds, or sparks, as they are termed in the Kabbalah, wished to pay back to The Supreme Intelligence, the Universal Self, for the *unconditional, unselfish* and *endless love* that It poured into them when endowing them with spirit and so, giving them existence. They were embarrassed by the fact that without any reason, their "Father" gave such a kind of love to them; something precious was being given undeservedly to them—like an unearned *bread*, bringing *disgrace* to the one eating it. Being so, they decided that the most suitable manner to return it would be to go **down** into matter, to 'descend' from the ultra refined spheres of pure spirit into the other, extreme end of the spectrum matter-spirit, there to live. Then, upon completion of this singular cycle, they would return to Father and pour their love to Him in their turn, earning His love by the existence in matter and all that it entails.

Another doctrine, the Theosophical, more or less similar in action to the Kabbalistic theory but differing in reason, states that The Supreme Intelligence disperses those seeds, emerging as sparks—using the Kabbalistic term—from Its Eternal Fire of Existence. This is done with the intent to immerse them in matter and reunite with them upon their return from it at the end of their ascension from there. Upon their descent into matter, the sparks incarnate, embracing a much denser material form, and then, reincarnate time after time in a cyclical fashion. Completing the number of cycles required—there are a few figures floating around as to what this number is, the most mentioned being 777, but this number is too alluding of the proverbial seven, so it may be a wishful thinking—they return to their source.

The Supreme Intelligence initiates this action for a specific reason: It wishes to enrich Itself with **all** the possible knowledge and information available in the Universe that It Itself created, expanding Its wisdom perpetually. This acquired education, shall we so call it, is accumulated during the experience gathered by the descending sparks during the reincarnation cycles. Upon their return to their source, The Supreme Intelligence, they pour it in Its lap, enriching It with yet another piece of personal wisdom and insight, and reunite with It.

The practicality of this cosmic approach will be apparent when the subject of *karma* will be explained in the course of the book.

The Awakening

The vast, and we may safely say the absolute majority of humanity is in a state of oblivion regarding this aspect of our existence, that is, the existence of Self in us, the disconnection and the alienation from it.

This state of oblivion can be, and in fact is, likened to a state of sleep, as mentioned in passing before. We need to be "awakened" to see the "light". This can happen with the aid of a drive or motivation that acts as trigger, internal or external. Such triggers, then, start a process of questioning and reasoning, which, if we persist in it, goes on and on in a cyclical pattern—questioning and reasoning and again, until a satisfactory answer is reached whether to embark on the Spiritual Way or not.

Some triggers may be direct and explicit, others can be sporadic, infrequent and unpremeditated, indirect and inexplicit, unconnected to the outcome that they inspire. They serve for what they are, only, just triggers, which, by way of some wild and unexplained, errant association, activate a dormant perception of the basic questions about our identity, our source, our task in this world and our heading. This book was purchased, probably, because of such a trigger, which started the process of questioning and reasoning.

The internal triggers are always direct and explicit, an insight that just happens then and there, a sudden comprehension of what is "going on".

The external triggers can be just about anything and everything. A falling leaf in the gentle autumn breeze or a word overheard from the table next to ours in a café can do the gentle, but momentous push. It can be an idea picked while attending a lecture, or while reading a book, any book.

There are many times when we do not even know, let alone remember, that a trigger had been released, awakening us, and so, starting the process of recognition of an innate, totally forgotten, familiar knowledge.

The Call

Now, of course, there are those, and they are many, who even when triggered, directly or indirectly, explicitly or not, internally or externally, will deny the validity of the glimpse that was just experienced. They will brush it aside, offhandedly, as something that is unimportant, something that is not to be pursued any further. In that case, their time has not come yet, as a basic tenet of Spirituality has it:

"When the Pupil is ready, the Teacher arrives"

For people who are not ready, these triggers will not be activated. They will not be transformed into teachers through the process of developing and assimilating them. When the pupil is ready, he allows the additional knowledge brought by the activated triggers to transcend his knowledge, his consciousness. Then, there is room in the person's awareness for this knowledge and for the teacher who will expound it, explaining it and guiding him on the spiritual road.

In the instances in which the triggers are acknowledged and, being conscious of them we wish to pursue them further, there arises a fundamental question: How do we know that they are "for real", that it will be right to hold on to them and to follow their pointing finger? How can we be sure that they are not just a voice that quite a few heard, a personal conviction, which, in so many instances, ended disastrously, and not because of some outer circumstances or factors, but because of the individual's own doing, or, rather, undoing?

"God told me", says the person; "I hear voices", declares another; "My intuition tells me I'm right", is trying he to convince others, and dreadful things happen. Yes, there is the Natural Infinite Wisdom on which we can depend, but an additional proof needs to be added when applying it to our own life and the lives of others.

In the last two or three decades of the 20th century, but not only, we had horrific examples of spiritual leaders who, because of their own misperceptions, misled their flock and drove them to commit terrible things to themselves and to others. Such leaders transformed the message into a cult and the group into a slavish following with little or nothing to say but with much to give to him, including their families and property and their own bodies and lives, literally.

Many such cults made use of verbal, mental, physical and sexual abuse against the group members, including children. They did such things against innocent and unsuspicious outsiders, too, including murder, the Sarin gas attack in Tokyo's subway net being a perfect example of such terrible acts in the name of spirituality.

There is an additional answer to the question of how

do we know that the call is true, besides the Natural Infinite Wisdom. Together, these pair of tools makes a perfect blend of justification. This additional tool is magnificent, the constant and unwavering use of which can reassure us of the authenticity of the triggers that awaken us.

The Law of Universal Love

Because of the inherent peril of following dangerous misperceptions, I cannot exaggerate and I cannot emphasize and be clear enough about the importance of discerning in simple and basic terms of *good* and *bad* what we want to do when we experience these insights. The decision should be strictly, clearly and unambiguously for adhering only to accepted basic norms of behavior and the formal law.

There is a very simple and basic way of knowing if we are on the **right, good** and **positive** track. In the world through which we go and in the life that we live, besides the Natural Infinite Wisdom that we possess inherently, there is a basic law that can help us to find the answer to this question. This is the Law of Universal Love.

This law will tell us with absolute certainty when we are right and when we are wrong. This statement is valid for any person having the basic normal faculty of distinguishing between good and bad. Any such person can apply this law and have an immediate answer.

The Law of Universal Love states in the most simple and concise manner:

"Love thy neighbor as thyself!"

In plain English, it would be "Don't do to someone else what you don't like yourself". Explained further, it says, "You don't like to be insulted and dishonored, right? You don't like your rights to be trespassed. Then don't do such things to another in your turn!" Simple. Basic. Straightforward.

The basic principle here, is that we have some instinctual likes and dislikes, all of which touch upon a very fundamental base of feelings. These feelings stem from an unadulterated wholeness, the core of our being from birth. This wholeness is a replica of The Self dwelling in its utter sanctity, derived from its absolute purity, and filtered through the physical matter in such a way as to be represented as closely as possible on this Earthly plane, but in terms comprehensible by the physical human being.

When this sacred core is violated, it is distorted in some way and it changes. The change evokes a feeling of abuse and mistreatment. Abused and mistreated, our wholeness has been tainted forever. We shall carry with us an unpleasant feeling in some measure or other, for the rest of our life. We may forgive the one who did it to us and forget it altogether but, in many instances, we do not forget it, and the bad feeling, though diminishing overtime stays with us forever.

The Resolution

Knowing this or having experienced such a thing, should bring us to the resolution that we shall not desecrate the sacred core of another, because we shall trespass and taint his sanctity forever. In doing so, we shall mistreat him and he will be left with a horrid, disagreeable feeling, all his life.

Do not ridicule, do not denigrate, do not insult and do not assault the other, verbally or physically. Do not do something that will inflict a wound to their body and to their soul. Never! Under any circumstances! I know, it is easier said than done, but let us, at least, try to behave that way. If we shall try consistently, maybe it will become a second nature to us and we shall live this commandment and fulfill it in our own lives. It is possible, I know it, I try it myself, and though I fail sometimes, maybe many times, other times I succeed. I know people who do it with an even greater measure of success. I know of wives who stay with grumpy husbands, I know of mothers and wives who stick with a stubborn loyalty to renegade husbands and children. I, as many others, heard of a certain Mother Teresa; I know of people who gave their lives to save others. Yes, it is possible.

None of us is expected to succeed in this endeavor every time we do it. We are expected, though, to **try** to succeed. If we would succeed every time we try, we would have been angels already and would not be here, right? But we are here and we are not angels yet, so try, try hard, try to do it always, remind yourself of this law always and by the bye it will become a second nature to you, tipping the balance between failures and successes to the scale of success.

Besides applying it to others, this law should be applied also to ourselves. To bear with the other and to forgive him should really start with us. We cannot but see ourselves in the other and the other in ourselves. If we bear with our mistakes and forgive ourselves for them, we shall find it easier to do the same to our neighbor, to the person next in line in the grocery store, to the driver next to us on the road, to the neighbor who makes this impossible noise on Sunday morning with this contraption, mowing the grass.

Even when angered by such "wrongdoings", we should not hate our neighbor or ourselves. Anger or upset should not be followed by hatred. Try to avoid these feelings, the upset and the anger, but once they appear, look at them as natural and perfectly acceptable, for indeed, we are only, and only humans. Do not carry them, though, to an upper level and into action, do not transform them into hatred.

Understanding it

Now, it will serve us well to understand The Law of Universal Love in all its wondrous simplicity and far-reaching and utterly positive consequences.

When Jesus Christ said in His infinite wisdom "Give the other cheek", "Give him your cloak, too", "Walk with him another mile", He meant, "Forgive him", "Help him", "Bear with him".

I, the little, am of the opinion that He did not mean literally to give our unslapped cheek when slapped on the other. He meant to forgive and go on, not to pursue a quarrel or a fight. For this proposed meaning, there is a logical and simple reason, which will be explained shortly.

I do not think that He meant that we go naked when another is deprived of some of his garments. Nor do I think that He meant that we should exhaust and reduce ourselves to nothing, when asked to help. He meant to help as much as we can in a situation of necessity for another, but in reasonable limits.

If, on the other hand, the issue is of a life and death import and only our life would save the other's, then we may choose to do so, of course, and it would certainly be extraordinary, awesome and inspiring beyond belief if someone goes to such unselfish extremes. Such acts of self-sacrifice are known in the history of humankind, but this is not what was intended in His teachings. For consider: What would be the point in losing one life just to save another solely? Why would be one life better than another when compared for their sanctity? Therefore, if such an act is contemplated, it should be weighed against the relative gain encountered, as materialistic as it may sound: If the sacrifice were surpassed by the eventual gain for the other, then such an act would be warranted. For example, if the person for whom the act of sacrifice is performed is a father who is the sole provider for a family, then the assistance offered by the sacrifice exceeds the limits of the one-on-one match of the helped and the helper. More than one person gained from it, and they gained in the long term. An undeniable act of ultimate instance of neighborly help was done. This is to be cherished forever, not to be forgotten, and, if one has the moral fiber necessary, for it demands utter spiritual fortitude and extreme bravery, even followed.

But, to my mind, besides the example above, which is a very out of common occurrence, Jesus meant to instruct us in our daily life that we would do well to forgive our neighbor and to bear with him, to help him in any way we can, but not to the point of self-obliteration. Why so? What is the rationale behind these directives, commandments, almost?

The reason for this lies in the fundamental knowledge of the human being's journey on Earth, through this valley of sorrow, and in the fact that this journey involves a continuous and advancing development for all of us.

As such, every one is in a different stage in this advancement, every individual is on a different step on this ladder of development. All we know is what was revealed to us in the particular stage in which we are and up to it only, not beyond. We do not know anymore than that, we may even know less, for that matter. We know what we were shown and taught and, very important, assimilated, which can be all that we were taught, part of it, or nothing at all. What we think, say and do is exactly what we know. If you were not taught that 2 X 2 = 4, you would think of 4 as the result of 2 + 2, only. You were taught only addition, not multiplication, so how in the world would you know that 4 can be the result of multiplying 2 by 2, also?

This being the situation, we are now in the point in which we can understand that when we did something wrong to someone, if he knew better he would not have slapped us, he would have only cursed. Had he known better yet, he would not even curse, but would keep silent and refraining from doing anything, knowing that what we did that aggravated him was only because this was what **we** knew. In the best of worlds, he would hug us in a brotherly love, telling us how we were wrong in doing what we did, as he would do to a little child, hoping that we would understand and improve our knowledge and so, our behavior.

If our little child broke the glass, we do not hit him, we do not even yell at him. If we are wise and compassionate, we try to put some wisdom in his little head and hope he will remember it. And little by little, he will.

Love one another; love your neighbor as yourself. This is the basic tenet of Spirituality.

The Law of Unity

Another reason for this basic precept of Universal Love, beyond the factor of the individual stage of development, is the definite reality that all of us are equally offspring of the Creation, no matter how each of us perceives this notion. You and I, he and everyone else, are here stemming from the same source. This is known as The Law of Unity, the basic law of the Creation, of which the Law of Universal Love is a first derivative.

Everything under heaven is part of the Creation, part of one whole, an integral piece of it, not to be severed. The only thing that holds it together, and, indeed, the only necessary thing for it, is the love that the Creator, the Universal Self, has for all that It created. Without this love, all will fall apart. This love radiates through the whole of Creation and permeates it, holding it in one piece; it is an endless, unconditional and unselfish kind of love. It does not ask to be loved in return and does not ask for something in return. It pours forth in an infinite and eternal flow, a cornucopia of love streaming from the fountainhead of the Creation, for the Creation.

It being so, it is apparent that we, all of us, are children of the same parent bound together by His love.

"We are unique in manifestation but universal in substance"

There is a common denominator binding us together in a tie that is not to be disconnected. As children of the same "father", we, all of us, are brothers and sisters. We are really one big family.

Be wise

Recognizing that you are part of this unity, and bound to it by this understanding, will you not help your brother? Will you not forgive your kin for doing things that you do not approve? Remember the times when you did the same and hoped you would be forgiven, put yourself in his shoes and try to understand him. Always try to understand and be compassionate, reasonable. To be reasonable one has to be wise, and this means to be able to display the fortunate cocktail of intelligence and compassion, love and understanding, the blend of wisdom.

Coming back full circle

So, the questions of how do we know if the trigger we experience is a right one and how do we know if we are on the right track, have an answer besides that given by our innate wisdom. We can say that if they are in accordance with The Law of Universal Love, then there should be no doubt in our mind of their soundness and authority. If they are not, then we should abandon them and the sooner the better, preferably immediately.

Following this exposure to the "light", generated by the various triggers, these insights come to the fore as an inner prodding that prompts us to take action in this particular regard. This is how this journey, the Quest for The Self, The Divine in us, starts.

A trigger started a process that initiated an insight that enlightens our consciousness, making us keenly aware of it. We are prompted to this by unconscious or unnoticed events in our daily life. Somehow, our attention is drawn to it. These insights and unnoticed events alert us to do something, which, in effect, reestablishes the lost awareness to our Self and the need to reconnect the disrupted link with it, and so, to reunite with it. We are going home.

Once we are on our way, it is highly desirable to make use of some tools to this end, tools, which, preferably, are the most potent and promising, the most efficient. This is where, in the next chapter, we shall direct our attention.

Chapter Two

The How and What of Spirituality – Walking the Way

...

How-to and with What

When people hear for the first time about Spirituality and that there are many who pursue it actively and in earnest, there are always some who express their interest in it and their wish to hear more about it. The inevitable question arises, then:

"How to do it and what is the best way".

The Approach

In this regard, there are, broadly speaking, two kinds of Seekers.

There are those who, once they decided to embark on this quest, follow one, and one rule, only, The Universal Law of Love. All they do is to apply in the circumstances of their everyday life the commandment *"Love thy neighbor as thyself"*. Sure enough, this is as much as necessary; after all is said and done, this is all that is really needed. Eventually, this kind of life purifies the mind and the soul, and, in the end, it purifies the body, too, because such a person reaches a point in which coarseness, in all its forms, cannot be suffered, he just cannot bear it.

For the rounded and polished, accomplished, spiritual-to-be person, however, there is a well-tested approach to attain The Self: Following an established method. It is advisable that this method would be one of the well-known and beaten paths on which we can pursue our quest.

There are quite a number of well-defined methods, each with its own band of adherents and sympathizers. However, it should be known that, ultimately, regarding any given genuine reality or hard fact, when stripped of the subjectivity of the personal point of view, then

> ***"For each Subject, there is only one Truth. The Number of Ways to it equals the Number of the Seekers of this Truth"*** (DB)

How can it be otherwise? In every domain, every question, there can be only one truth, by definition. There can be different points of view regarding a truth, but, ultimately, all of them observe the same thing.

Each viewer, each Seeker, has his personal nuances and idiosyncrasies, each his personal characteristics and peculiarities, his personal approaches and inclinations. This is what accounts for the different points of view, the diversity of the minds observing the specific truth. There may be similar points of view among different individuals but, as a rule, we hold, mostly, different views. Making their way to the truth, the Seekers will ultimately meet at the same point, the sole, unadulterated, definitive truth, but they, each one of them, tread their uniquely individual way.

The vast majorities of Seekers, unique as they might be in their own personal approach, converge in greater groups and make use of one of the well-known methods, with its specific techniques and tools.

Each one of these methods uses tools that affect the Seeker physically and mentally, as well as emotionally and spiritually.

While seeking for such a method, suitable for the unique **YOU**, some ideas and notions that you shall be taught and to which you shall be exposed, will appear a little strange and uncommon. This is so because, as a rule, they are not part of the conventional frame of mind and the accepted wisdom. These spiritual approaches started to make inroads into the conventional thinking only recently, and because of the broad exposure that everything is given now, in this age of open and global communication, many of us are familiar in some measure or other with some of the ideas of Spirituality, and even with some of its jargon. Yet, when trying to study and apply them, one might be surprised a little because of what may seem odd to an untrained ear.

All the ideas expounded in these methods and the means that are used, are empirical, except for a specific subject: the explanations given to the creation of the Universe and its shape and structure, labeled as Cosmology. Almost every method and school has its own different explanation, which is abstract and speculative.

Regarding these empirical methods, disciples of Spirituality, novices and adepts alike, tried and erred in various approaches and used different techniques and methods during thousands of years, literally, in many places. Thus, all the methods about which we hear and read, represent an endless and tenacious attempt on the part of humanity, through its most advanced and enlightened individuals, to accomplish one and one thing only, namely to regain the lost connection to The Self in the individual human being and to reunite with it. Through it, then, to be one with the higher Self, The Universal Self.

As a direct result of this, not surprisingly so, one can find echoes of a particular technique in other methods and other schools, under different names. Drawing from it a logical conclusion it can be safely said that, no matter which school or method is adopted, if one is determined to walk The Way and perseveres in it, he will eventually attain his goal, finding The Self and reuniting with it. All he has to do is to pursue it in earnest and, eventually, in a way that fits him and his needs, his uniqueness.

Do not be afraid to acquaint yourself with different theories. Try the one that suits you best according to your personal inclinations and preferences and current development. Then, do not be afraid to discard it when you outgrew it or found that it does not strike a chord in your inner world, anymore.

You shall always outgrow a technique, finding that it no longer helps you as it was in the beginning, when you started to employ it. Even so, some basic tools and techniques will stay with you forever. For example, *meditation*, the most basic tool of them all, will remain indispensable, at least in its fundamental concept.

When you do not resonate in unison with a technique or a method or school, this is the time to part ways and try something else.

No theory and no individual may claim that they have all the answers, including this author; therefore, by trying a number of them, you shall gather different points of view, which, together, will provide a fuller answer to your goals, questions and doubts.

By the very fact that the number of ways to the truth equals the number of seekers for it, every method will attempt to answer the questions that the founder or initiator of this method posed, and so, basically, the answers are limited to those questions. By the very fact that some reject other methods and adhere to one only, we can understand that those other approaches did not satisfy them, and so, they discarded them. Yet, it is possible that there can be an answer to something of interest to us in almost every method or school. We should not dismiss them outright on the face of it, unless they present a basic flaw, according to our basic standards and principles.

Every method and school has something of interest to offer. There is not a book, there is not a theory or a method, in which we shall not be able to find a new aspect or a new meaning, different from what we knew just a minute ago, so try until you find something that appeals to you.

Following this short description of the commonality of methods and of the manner of how to approach them, there are a few general but very important initial instructions that should be followed faithfully, if efficient and lasting accomplishments are desired.

Preliminary instructions before coming aboard, call for a correct *attitude*, a *teacher* and the *right kind of pursuit*. They are of an imperative necessity. If followed, they will ensure a structured and steady advancement on the path we chose to tread. In this manner, we can be sure that the aspired development and accomplishment will come.

Attitude

The first preliminary instruction deals with "*Correct Attitude*". Without it, we miss the mark.

Openness of mind, a receiving vessel that is empty, and lack of any prejudices, should be the qualities of our attitude when we adopt a method, any method, to show us The Way; in fact, this dictum is suitable for any kind of learning.

An open mind is a mind that is willing to listen to anyone who has something to say, and, for that matter, to listen always, for there is a message in everything we encounter. Not being open to listen, turns us deaf to any sound, much to our detriment, and this, of course, is to be avoided. We have to listen with all our being, intently, not only with our ears. In everything around us, there is a note that can strike a cord in us, and many times will.

"Teacher, please teach me all you know!" asked the young man.

The old man smiled with endless love and wisdom, and, after going away for a few moments, he came back and offered the young man tea.

Content and happy, the young man looked at the old man pouring the tea.

The old man poured until the cup was almost full, and kept pouring. The cup was full. He did not stop even then, and kept pouring. The tea spilt into the saucer and the old man kept pouring. The young man looked with astonishment at the sight of such apparent folly.

"But teacher, the cup is full!" said the young man with much surprise, "Why do you keep on pouring?"

"See? This is how you are now, full as this cup of tea. You think that you already know it all. I cannot pour into you another drop of knowledge", said the teacher.

An empty bowl should accompany this openness, for even if we are willing to listen to everything, if the bowl is full, not one drop of what we hear will stay in. We are the bowl. When we think that we know everything, we are full, and though we may *hear* well the whole range of sounds the Creation has to offer us in all its diversity, we shall not pay the necessary attention because we do not *listen*. We may be so preoccupied with the belief that "we know it all" that the message will not be absorbed and processed. When we are full, the world around us is only a constant unintelligible background noise, a chitter-chatter, so put your books and notebooks aside and make room for a new idea. Then, the noise humming outside will be meaningful.

In learning, there is no place for narrow-mindedness, as there is no place for it anywhere. In order to process correctly all the messages to which we open ourselves, our approach to analyze and intuit them should lack any preconceptions we may entertain. We should discard any previous rules of measure that we used to apply to the world surrounding us. They act like brakes on the personal development.

An open, blank and fair mind and heart shall bring us far, very far. The whole world and its horn of plenty shall be ours. Listen, just listen. Completely new vistas will open before your eyes. The world around you will be broader, farther, higher.

Teacher

The second general advice, but, this time, a more specific one, is that The Way cannot be covered fully and efficiently without the aid of a teacher, an instructor, known in the spiritual circles as "guru", a word borrowed from Hindu spirituality.

The meaning of the word is "destructor (gu) of darkness (ru)"—implying that the teacher destroys the darkness of our ignorance through his knowledge. In most cases, only through the aid of an instructor can an honest Seeker walk the way successfully.

The reason for this is that the knowledge gained through one's own efforts is helpful only partially, because it relies on one's own ability to "see through". Since this ability is related directly to one's spiritual development, it is obviously limited in its capacity, especially when the Seeker is a novice.

A Seeker who relies on his own efforts, finds himself in a vicious circle, in which, in order to develop further, he puts himself at the mercy of his current development. In such a case, additional development is possible, of course, but, in most cases, it will be weak and limited, and it may cause inner friction. A self-instructed Seeker is like a blind man groping around to find his way in the darkness. He may find it, eventually, but he may not, and in any case, even if successful, he will encounter many obstacles, causing frustration, doubt and reversals.

The guiding and the instructions of a teacher who is already ahead on The Way, give a sense of order and direction to the process and help in assessing the development of the pupil at any given time.

Since the spiritual process involves an entire personal metamorphosis through a whole mental and psychical transformation, there is a possibility of mental and psychological harm to the Seeker. This possibility is real and everyone undertaking this quest is warned against it. We shall come back to this risk in due time, in Ch. Seven, in the section "Benefits and Pitfalls...". The guiding of a genuine and good teacher would make it easier to prevent such harm.

Moreover, and this is perhaps the most important thing, since the teacher, in his turn, is connected to higher teachers, the bond with him ensures that the disciple is connected too, eventually, to those higher intelligences. This is one of the best ways through which we, as active seekers, are able to encounter the Great Teachers, the Messiahs of all times, and be embraced by them.

The ancient Hindu scriptures describe the bond between the disciple and his teacher explicitly, without giving room to the smallest doubt, as a bond of absolute devotion and obedience on the part of the disciple towards the teacher.

In those modern times and in the West in particular, such a bond is maybe hard to find or establish in the broad society, but even there, there are many examples to show that it is perceived as an ultimate requisite and exercised in many places.

This is the case in all the established religions. The Pope, the head of the Roman Catholic Church, the Chief Rabbi in

Israel, the Imams and Ayatollahs of the Islamic Sunni and Shiite faiths, the Dalai Lama of the Tibetan Buddhism, the Rabbi heading any Hassidic Jewish sect, all are proper examples of this demand.

Though not recommendable for the obvious reasons, various cults beside the established religions make this subject one of utmost importance and they demand absolute obedience and loyalty to the leader of the cult. Such a leader presents himself as all-knowing and his word is final.

This bond is the all-important thing, almost, in the teacher–disciple relationship. In the daily life, though, this relationship is not so rigid; it is, probably, more dynamic and there are many degrees of involvement to be found between a teacher and his disciples.

I would venture and say that a serious Seeker would choose to go to a suitable place to follow closer, more intensively, a method and a teacher. Such a Seeker will join an "ashram" in India, or a Zen monastery in Japan. He can join a Christian seminar or monastery, or a Jewish "yeshiva".

There is no difference between a spiritual quest in itself and a religious one. Both have the same goal, to find the Divine and to make It the Lord of our lives. The perceptions and the ways to achieve it are different but all meet in the end in the same place, the bliss and the enlightenment following its discovery and the union with it.

The committed Seeker dedicates himself to a certain belief and way of life and to the head of this school at the time.

Pursuit

The last general instruction involves the kind of pursuit the Seeker should conduct.

No less important than the other two approaches, *attitude* and *teacher*, the *pursuit* for The Self should be relentless, made into an inseparable part of our daily conduct and followed incessantly ad infinitum. Our activities and behavior should follow and reflect as closely as possible the precepts of spirituality in all aspects of life.

We should follow our pursuit in earnest. Every pursuit in life should be taken in earnest if we want good and lasting results, and this particular pursuit, the Quest for The Divine, ten times over. It is to be done with maximum seriousness and with the greatest determination, in a permanent and sustained manner. The one who will make it to the end of the spiritual road is the dedicated Walker, not the uncommitted.

It is a well-known maxim in all spiritual traditions that, in the end, one becomes the thing on which he is focusing his attention. The author defines it thusly:

"You are what you are at" (DB)

meaning that if you give your undivided attention to a blade of grass, then you are there, with this grass blade, you are in it, and you **are** the grass blade.

The attention is measured in terms of concentration and dedication. The measure of the concentration and dedication to the object at hand, defines the rules of engagement: The more concentrated you are in what you do, the more involved you are with it, and vice versa, the more involved you wish to be with someone or something, the more concentration and dedication you have to put into it.

Dedication to the object at hand is the conscious effort we make to be concentrated in whatever kind of relationship we wish to establish with it. This conscious effort can be interpreted aptly in the light of the maxim of old,

"Die and be reborn!"

When you strive consciously to concentrate on whatever preoccupies you, you *die* in regard to yourself and are *reborn* anew in the thing that requires your attention and to which you dedicate it.

In itself, this object is always out of **you**, out of the bounds of your immediate personal cognitive awareness, **you** being the worldly ego representing the person that you are "in the world". In order to make yourself aware of this thing, you have to "offer" to it some of you, directing to it some of your cognitive faculties.

This "out-of-your-personal-bounds" object to which you address your awareness, can be anything and everything. It can be the very thing you do now, the person you think about this moment or the project with which you are currently involved. In our context, it is The Self. The associative explanation is simple: Since we lost connection with it, The Self can be defined, now, as an "out-of-personal-bounds" object.

Following the maxim above, to make something out there "yours", you have to "die" to yourself, even a little bit. You give a "little bit of yourself" to this "something", and then, it is yours in a certain measure. Therefore, **nothing** is "yours" unless you put something of yourself in it. The basic personal perception that "this is mine" only because I own it, is but an illusion. In order to be able to say "I own it" and to feel the ownership, we have to yearn for it, at least a little. In order to yearn for it, we have to feel the wish to make it ours, at least a little. Then, reciprocally, when "a bit of you" is in "the whole of it", "it" owns you, too. This is not a one-directional street; it is bi-directional.

The act of giving a part of you to someone or for something, is an act of self-renunciation.

In everyday life, you may give of yourself as much as you like, or as little as you like.

In the quest for The Self, this renunciation has to be maximal. The more we give of ourselves, our worldly self, to it, the more the lost connection with it is regained and the more we are reconnected with it. To regain it wholly, we must, simply, give ourselves wholly.

This measure of reconnection is determined directly by the measure of dedication we are willing to grant to it. Since the measure of dedication determines the measure of concentration we employ, then the more dedicated we are in this pursuit, the more concentrated we are in it.

This is the reason why the quest for The Self should be taken in all earnest and be a permanent one. Such attitude is dedication and this is what should define the pursuit in which we are engaged.

Lessons

Let us materialize, now, the general instructions presented above and see how we can apply them in our pursuit.

We employ the right *pursuit* and *attitude*. We look for a *teacher*. We found him. How do we know, now, if the teacher we met and with whom we are about to shake hands, is a good and genuine one?

Calling the ancient Hindu scriptures again to help us in such questions, we find that they define such a teacher, among other things, as one versed in the scriptures, a devotee of God, free from envy and pure.

A true teacher is also one who is more advanced on the way, in every aspect that matters. He is significantly ahead of the pupil and can give good and useful lessons to him.

However, besides the formal teacher, life can teach us too. As said before, anything and everything can be a teacher, for if we care to listen, in each instance, in each place and thing coming our way, there is a lesson we can learn. We should adopt a proper approach to the teachings of life, meaning listening to anyone, listening attentively, willingly, even when this person is the exact antipode of the lesson conveyed by or through him: A thief will tell you that it is bad to steal. Would you not listen to him just because he is a thief and stole an apple just a moment ago? A prostitute will tell you that she is a sinner, a bad woman; will you not listen to her just because the very next minute she gave herself to a perfect stranger for money?

Actually, this is something that happened to me on my way to a spiritual meeting, of all things. Evening fell, already. I had to walk through a street known for this trade at night. Passing a woman who evidently was there for this purpose, I told her that what she was doing was not good. Not good in itself and not good for her, and I added a few other educational, reformative remarks. I did so entirely unsolicited. What came over me, I do not know until this very day. I just felt at that moment that I had to reach her soul, the dignified human being in her. I felt driven, I was on a mission. Nonetheless, I was fully aware of the fact that her pimp might come any moment and give **me** a lesson that I might never forget. The thought never left me, but I did not mind it. She listened quietly, without making any objections, and then, she asked me rhetorically, affirming it, "I'm bad, ain't I?" "In what you're doing, yes", I said. Nevertheless, she gave herself in that very second to someone who just came and chose her.

I am sure that, if given the opportunity, she would have given me an unforgettable lecture about how appalling and degrading was what she was doing.

So, in spite of the good potential lesson, should I not listen to her because she was inconsistent, because she was not following her own correct assessment of her situation and the implied advice? I think I should listen. And I did. I listened to the rhetorical, affirmative lone question of hers, with much respect.

In such instances, what is important is the lesson, not the appearance or the substance of the one who gives it, so we ought to listen to anyone, to anything.

The bird in the sky can be a teacher; the cloud framing the flying bird can be a teacher; the wind and the grass with which the bird plays and which it nibbles can be teachers. Every memory and every cognitive action can act as teachers. Our five senses can be wonderful teachers by triggering sensations, which, in turn, trigger feelings, triggering thoughts in their turn.

These sensations, feelings and thoughts, are the lessons we are taught every moment of our life by everything that happens to us.

We can learn life's lessons in two ways: accidentally, by chance, or systematically, in a predetermined and methodic way.

The Talmud, one of the most important Jewish scriptures, says that everyone learns in the end

"By the law of the land or by the way of the teachings"

Any path we take in life has its own laws, rules and measures.

If we take a path unknowingly or blindly, whatever happens along the way will be accidental for us and we may stumble upon some incidents with a measure or other of detrimental results, unless some coincidence occurs and we are not harmed.

In the accidental way, life itself, in all its occurrences, goads and pushes us from behind to do something or to behave in a certain way. In such instances, we are reacting to the lessons of life and, in so doing, we learn what is there to know, the very rules that we may have trespassed, *the laws of the land* in the above maxim.

On the other hand, if we were taught the rules beforehand, which is the *way of the teachings* mentioned above, then we would be conscious of the way in which we conduct our life because we would have to consider them. Yes, there are always those who disregard the laws, but they would be the out of common that would prove the common.

In this regard, the spiritual lessons are not different from the lessons of life, and they too can be learned haphazardly or methodically.

As individuals who aspire to evolve spiritually, we should choose to go through life methodically, with the initiative in our hands, not in a reacting way.

A systematic approach to our journey on this earthly plane will put us in control of ourselves and, ultimately, in control of our circumstances, inasmuch as our present incarnation life-plan accomodates it.

When we walk The Way and try to follow its precepts, whatever they are in the specific school and method we practice, we are like a boat equipped fully: We have a compass and a sail, a keel and a rudder. In the frame of our abilities and surrounding circumstances, we are in control of the direction to which we are heading and of the speed with which we sail. We are no longer in a bare nutshell floating on the water, helpless victims to the wind and the waves.

Walking The Way systematically, will be, after a while, as natural and effortless to us as breathing.

Let us have an example of doing or not doing something in an accidental way or through a systematic learning of the rules that govern conduct: I do not steal.

Now, I may not steal because of three possible reasons, two of them external and one, internal: I was born with this trait of character, or, I was taught the other two. Let us see how each of them is unfolding, potentially.

The internal reason is a trait of my character from birth. I just cannot do it, so I do not steal, period. This is, obviously, the best reason of all. I learnt somehow, in previous lives, probably, that stealing is something that one does not do. When born in this life, I already had it: "I do not steal". It is with me and this is what I am: I have brown eyes, brown hair, and I do not steal; it is an inherent trait of my being, built-in.

The other two, external reasons, I was taught, so they are of an acquired nature. One is fear, the other is knowledge; if assimilated fully, both reasons will lead in a future life to the first, internal reason for not stealing, the trait of character mentioned above.

The fear-based reason rests on the fact that I shall be thrown in prison if caught stealing, and, oh my God, in some places, my right arm will be cut, even. Now that hurts. Bad, very bad!

The knowledge-based reason comes from the way I was taught by my parents and by the society in which I lived, or by one of them.

So, between the two instances of external reasons, which is more advanced? It will go without saying, I think, that it will be the one in which we are taught not to steal.

The one who fears that his arm will be dog-meat if caught stealing, is goaded not to steal by the life's hard facts, by the law of the land. He does so accidentally. He is reacting to the pushes and the spurs of life. If not for fear of punishment, he would steal unabashed.

The other one, the one who does so because this is the way he was **taught** to behave, is instilled with the imperative "You shall not steal" until it becomes part of his understanding and so, part of his conscious knowledge and of his awareness. This is something that is, and will be his, forever. In an extreme case, he may not heed it, but he will always be aware of it, whatever he does: "Do not steal", as a social imperative, will ring in his ears always.

Only after we **know** something, can we consider it as part of our awareness, our consciousness. Only then is this "something" ours. We put something of ourselves in it, remember? It became part of our bank of knowledge, our wisdom.

One way of knowing is to study the subject, to understand it and to assimilate it. Another is the intuitive one, the notion of "grasping" the subject, "getting, digging" it, about which we talked in the first chapter as The Infinite Natural Wisdom. Although in many instances both of them lead to knowledge, in spiritual matters the later is more valid than the first, for the very reason that we deal with transcendental subjects. However, even then, it is good to explore them, to turn them over and over again, to look at them from every possible angle until we understand all the nuances and all the various meanings.

When trying to know something, the *correct attitude* would be helpful. Being an open, empty vessel, and unbiased toward whatever pieces of information our investigation uncovers, ensures that we consider everything and that we do not leave anything unexplored.

Whatever the knowledge we gain and decide to make part of our toolbox, we shall *pursue* it with the appropriate seriousness discussed in "Pursuit", above. We shall dedicate our whole being to it and concentrate ourselves in what we do, in the best way we can.

The Toolbox

There are numerous tools and means from which to choose and employ in our quest. Besides other, well-known and broadly accepted ones that are in the spiritual "public" domain, like meditation, for example, every school develops its own tools, so the Seeker may find in any school to which he attaches himself some that are common, and others that are specific to that particular school. However, even the common tools can be different from school to school in these or other nuances, like emphasis on different points, order of practicing different stages, etc.

Quite a few of the tools presented here can be found in the approach that people who are far from being involved in the search for spirituality, apply to the whole range of humanity's problems in its daily life.

The difference is that their attempts to find answers, and the use of these tools for their goal, do not come from a spiritual point of view. Their specific and conscious aim is dissimilar to the spiritual quest.

The quest for The Self anchors the human being in the spiritual, while at the same time recognizes him as the place where The Self, the focus of this search, resides; it recognizes it as its temple.

The secular quest for answers to the human condition, be it lay or academic, but not spiritual, places the human being in a predetermined way in the center of a surrounding world of matter. From this place, it enables it to condition and manipulate matter at will, while in the same time it does not recognize any transcendent and primary source to them both, man and matter; in fact, it negates it. In other words, in this approach, what the senses perceive is the only thing there is to the expense of everything else, and from this, with this and for this, the human being is to proceed and succeed. Such a secular quest is trying to find the answers to the fundamental questions that every inquisitive mind is asking and the compass to finding the way in this world, by looking at the matter in which it lives as the sole source of existence and of the perceptions of the surrounding universe.

Regardless, in addition to specific spiritual tools, we shall elaborate upon some such "lay" tools in a spiritual context also, using them for our benefit. They can serve a dual purpose—secular and spiritual.

Trying to make some sense and order in this toolbox, we can generally speak about two kinds of tools: abstract and concrete. The abstract ones can be defined as *attitudinal means*; the concrete ones are *practical means*. They will be classified as means that should be employed or avoided. I do not attempt to define the tools to be employed as "indispensable", because there are people, as mentioned in the beginning of this chapter, who do not employ any tool whatsoever, except one, the most wonderful and efficient of them all, *Love,* brotherly and universal love, so nothing is indispensable as such. However, if, for some reason, such a simple and basic spiritual way is hard to carry out, or we wish to do more than that so we shall be able to develop ourselves in an orderly and systematic mode, it is desirable to know about as many tools and means as possible. Acquainting ourselves with them, we are, then, able to decide which ones to choose and to employ. This decision will reflect our personal inclinations, of course, but it will always be in accord with the existing laws, rules, mores and norms prevalent in our society and community. To this, there can be no exception, and I cannot emphasize it enough. Likewise, as dictated by the Law of Universal Love, we choose only tools that do not infringe upon the dignity and the physical well-being of our neighbor and of ourselves. Following these basic principles, you should follow your common sense. Associate yourself only with a teacher, a method or a school that adheres strictly to the practice of Universal Love as the underlying rule of their teachings.

Of the many means available to the spiritual seeker and known to me, I chose to bring before you only some of them, the ones that seem to me the most effective and important.

Some of them you met already in the first chapter, like The Law of Universal Love. I am sure that you took notice of them for what they are, tools to use on your spiritual way. Some of them will be mentioned again to clarify things in the appropriate context, or in passing; others will be found in the following chapters. Besides a short dissertation here, the theme of meditation is given a place of its own, the better part of this book, but the bulk of the tools will be found here.

You shall find that in many cases they echo each other, in some kind of repetition, an overlapping of sorts. This is so because all of these tools are closely interrelated and, in some measure or other, interdependent, so, in some cases, it is necessary to mention a principle while referring to another, or to repeat common features. The context will tell you how the relationship is founded and on what. Because of this, they are not listed in any particular order, except the first three.

Read them again and again, try to look at them from every possible angle; doubt them; compare them with other things you know. Not one word here, not one letter, is protected from being analyzed in depth. Dissect, and then reassemble them. Put them aside, and then, come back to them again. Above all, be open, receptive and unbiased. **Know** them.

Resources

Attitudinal Means

Of the many tools that will be mentioned here, there are three that their importance and specific weight set them apart from the others. They are, in order of importance, The Law of Universal Love, The Measure of Non-Attachment and The Eternal Present Approach. After elaborating at length on them, others, lesser but important too, will be presented. Let us start with the most important of them all,

The Law of Universal Love

Though explained already at length in Chapter One, this commandment is so significant that I shall mention it briefly again here through some different aspects, as the first in the series.

If there were one means, one device to be advised as The one to follow and employ, it would be this one. This law goes down through the ages in all societies as "Love thy neighbor as thyself" or some other similar expression, such as "Do not do unto others, as you would not have them done unto you".

We are Daughters and Sons of the Creation, and as such, we are brothers.

Everything done to another is done to ourselves, ultimately, and vice-versa. Showing love, understanding and empathy to our neighbor, will be in accord with this law. Treating another in an opposite way would be in disagreement with it.

When in doubt, we should put ourselves in the other's place. Then, if we feel that such an action would lower our vibrations, in other words, that it would hurt us in some way, then we are in disagreement with this law. A normal and decent person will feel a natural honest remorse when acting in disagreement with this law, because of the innate brotherhood felt instinctively for everyone else. The one who walks the spiritual way in earnest will feel so even more, because it will be felt consciously. The inflictor will feel acutely the wound inflicted unto another. Similarly, when we treat *ourselves* incorrectly, we feel a distinct sense of shamefulness, because of the very same reasons. We wounded our sacred core. In addition to the personal aspect, we perceive ourselves intuitively as an integral part of humanity, representing it, as if we were all the others combined. Treating ourselves not according to this law makes us feel "bad" because we hurt ourselves, and so, it was as though we hurt the others, too. Acting in accordance to this universal law in regard to us and others, makes us feel in harmony with the whole of creation. This is true even if we acted so only toward one other individual. Concerning this, the Talmud says thusly:

"He who saves one soul, it is as if he saved the whole world"

One person equals the whole world; the way we act toward him is synonymous with acting toward the whole world – The Law of Unity and its first derivative, The Law of Universal Love, are shown in full blossom here.

The Measure of Non-Attachment

An old monk and his young disciple made their way to the shallow waters of the river crossing, not far away. As they were coming closer to the river, they could hear a woman crying. Upon reaching the riverbank, they saw a young woman standing there looking at the water and crying, her bag on the ground.

"What is the matter, young woman, why are you crying?" the old monk asked her.

"I cannot cross the river, venerable one".

"Don't worry", he answered, "I'll bring you to the other side and all will be all right!"

Said and done. He carried her piggyback, and together, the three of them crossed the river safely. Reaching the other side, the monk put the woman down, and the two monks went their way. After a while, the young disciple turned to the old monk and asked:

"Venerable one, how is it that you took the woman on your back? We vowed for a life of celibacy, we are forbidden to touch a woman".

"Young man, can't you see? I put her down a long time ago but you still carry her".

Striving for a behavior in which attachment has no place, is a permanent tactical goal for the spiritual seeker. Let us see why this is so.

Attachment means connection, some kind of bond to an object, abstract or concrete. This kind of behavior involves body, feelings and thoughts; it is physical, emotional and mental. Let us explore this further.

Longing, desiring, are a kind of connection with the desired object or person. Therefore, desiring something will lead to an attachment to this subject. "*Desiring*" denotes, and produces always, an attachment. Attachment occurs when we expect results to our actions, also. Therefore, we can be attached to a subject or to the results of our actions. We shall detail this second type of attachment, the one to the results of our actions, in *Affirmations*, in the passage dedicated to *Prayers,*

Invocations and Affirmations, below. Now, let us concentrate on attachment to different subjects.

There are many kinds of attachment. When we drool over the ice cream we could not buy, this is attachment. Missing the loved one is attachment. Wanting titles, honors, degrees, riches, power, causes attachment. Our upbringing forms attachment to what we were taught and toward which we were conditioned. Fear of change means attachment to the old form: Doing the same old thing, even when there is an obvious need for change, is an attachment to an old habit, old pattern. Compulsion means extreme attachment: Doing something because of someone or something else, even when it is not necessary, is an attachment to the compelling person or object. Being unable to move about freely because of someone or something, no matter how positive this someone or something may be, no matter how lofty, is an attachment.

Attachment is always negative, because it inevitably brings sorrow in its wake. The longing in itself, the desire for the wanted subject, causes a state of expectation for the fulfillment of this craving. Most of our attention and efforts, and, in extreme cases, all of them, are directed toward this hope most of the time, or even constantly, not allowing room for anything else. The attention and the efforts are subjected to the overwhelming oppressive obsession caused by the craving for the certain object and to the expectation aroused in us for its anticipated realization, the satisfaction of our wish, crowned with its own hope. Anything else is felt and done offhandedly, in the background, stripped of its individual importance, because it is not paid attention for itself, being relegated to a secondary place. It is hard for us to wait for the fulfillment of this craving. We measure the seconds, not only the minutes. When the satisfaction of our wish is postponed, not to mention unfulfilled, we are sad and upset, frustrated and disappointed. In short, we suffer.

The situation in which we find ourselves when in a state of attachment, denies, in some measure or other, the freedom of body, mind and spirit. Therefore, even when the subject of attachment is a positive one, the consequences of the attachment will be negative because it makes us suffer; it hurts us, hampering our personal freedom.

However, though attachment causes suffering, it is a basic human state of mind and spirit. This is how we were made. We were born with it. We are in this world and we have to live in it, and maybe this is one of the tools given to us at birth to cope with it in an immediate and intimate way. Yet we do not have to remain forever in this situation, going through all the sorrow accompanying it without, at least, trying to improve our lot. There is a solution to it, which is simple, and certainly applicable, but, admittedly, not an easy one, sort of easier said than done. After a while, though, exercising it, you will get used to it eventually, making it easier, like a trained muscle that gets stronger all the time, making it easier to lift and to move heavier and heavier burdens.

The solution for this basic state of affairs of ours is not to repress the desire, not to resist it, but not to linger on it one unnecessary moment, either. Let us feel all we want, let us feel intensely, with all our heart, let us yearn for titles and honors, let us wait for the phone call from our lover, but let us not, **let us not** take it with us to bed when we go to sleep; it is a lousy bed companion. Let us not take it with us to the next moment of our life. Let us leave it right there and then, where it was born and when we felt it. Not a minute of peace of mind should be spoiled, not a bite of a good dish should stick in our throat and not a minute of restful sleep should go wasted because of it. It is okay to feel, it is okay to want, to yearn and to crave; it is perfectly legitimate, because it is in our nature, in our makeup. It is not okay, though, to linger on it if we are interested in our worldly wellbeing and happiness, and more so, in the spiritual. Feel and wish as much as you want, but do not take it with you. Detach yourself from it the minute it shows itself. Look at it from an impersonal distance. Go on with your life as if nothing happened. Do not shed a drop of tear for the call that did not come. Do not feel sorry for yourself for not getting this title you wanted, the honor you expected, all of which you think are yours, or should be yours, by right. Do not, because nothing happened, really. Nothing happened, because you are whole *with* or *without* **all** of them. You are the same person as you were before and you shall remain the same person afterward, receiving it or not. And most important, nothing bad happened because feelings are an essential ingredient in the spiritual development.

"The advancement on the spiritual path is faster if we listen to the feelings"
(DB)

Feelings are on a higher level than the physical and therefore they should be pursued, but intelligently and with common sense. Do not turn yourself into a slave of theirs; put them to work **for** you, let them not turn **against** you. Therefore, by all means, acknowledge your feelings, let them have their rightful part in your world, but do what you have to do, go on with your life, do it courageously, looking straight and far, holding your head high. You shall do it once, and twice, and ten times, and then, detaching yourself from the negative, and sometimes harmful, devastating influence of the bonds of attachment of any kind, will become a second nature to you.

"Dhammapada", a summary of Buddha's teachings, says thusly about it:

"Give up anger, renounce pride and overcome all bonds. He, who clings not to mind and body and is detached, never suffers".

The Approach of the Eternal Present

Time, in its three manifestations, *past, present and future,* has an important role in our lives.

The *past* is a significant part of our personal and individual legacy. It plays an important role in defining an important dimension of our life, namely who we are, that is, our identity. However, in the spiritual context, it presents a problem. The memories of the past preoccupy us constantly; they are with us always. In the light of the previous point, the Non-Attachment, this is something we should try to avoid. Thoughts, questions, reflections, ring in our head, all the time. "Why did that happen? And why did that happen as it happened? Was it all right what I said? Was it all right what I did?" We linger over them, unwilling to let them go, turning them over and over in our mind, like a song stuck there, buzzing all day long.

The *future* is the place where we store our intentions, our yet immaterialized plans. It is an unknown realm and will remain so forever. For us, it is a thing, a place that we are unsure of its presence and of its nature. We always worry about it and understandably so: "Will tomorrow be here, uh..., tomorrow?" Except for soothsayers, and even they make mistakes, we cannot know it beforehand. The future is veiled before our eyes and hides itself behind an impenetrable curtain. We are unsure of its substance and traits, unsure if it will be as we wish it to be or not. Moreover, our experience teaches us that our expectations of the future, based on certain, more or less logical assumptions, can change drastically, and sometimes negatively, in seconds, without any advance warning. Will our world be the same tomorrow? No one knows, really.

Surrounded by the physical world in which we live and influenced by it in everything that we do, we apply our cognitive and perceptive faculties in the frame defined by its dimensions, Time and Space. They can be powerful habituations, these two, acting on us like conditioners. Time and Space define the borders of all our undertakings, the When and the Where of our lives.

Time, the fourth dimension of the physical world in which we live is an ever-flowing river, beginning from the creation of the cosmos and ending with it, if it will ever end. (For the sake of being entirely explicit, the other three are the Space dimensions, the Cartesian coordinates of length, width and height, which determine the position of an object in space.)

From what we can gather from our vantage point in the material world in which we dwell, *time* is eternal, an ever pointing finger toward the future.

This defines the situation in which the physical world finds itself and will ever be.

In the Spiritual realm, however, in the purely energetic essence of the Universe, though, the only existing kind of time is, for want of a better word, the Present, and, by definition, this is an *eternal* Present, more correctly defined as a *non*-flowing kind of time. This type of time incorporates the parts known to us, past, present and future, in a singular, undifferentiated, inclusive unit.

As spiritual aspirants, we strive to be in **this** kind of Universe, we strive to be in the Eternal Present.

The question, now, is how do we do it, not if we can, because we certainly can. As the previous toolbox item, the Measure of Non-Attachment, this tool is simple and feasible also, but it also is easier said than done, no doubt. However, to be in a state of mind of Eternal Present, like Non-Attachment, demands only to train ourselves for it, and after some time, we shall be accustomed to it, so that it will be a second nature for us.

"Leave the present behind, making it your past, every time you step into the future. Care about the future, only when you are there. Then, it is the present of your life" (DB)

You will note that I used the term *care*, not *worry*. Worrying does not exist in the Spiritual Seeker's vocabulary. At least, we should try in all earnest to avoid this plague of mind and spirit, the worry, which mars one's peace of mind undeservedly.

Back to the precept, the above maxim is all there is to it, all you have to do; and doing it consciously, being fully aware of it.

However, in this world, for it to be a past and a future, there has to be a present, and this is where we always are, actually. Seen from the point of view of the dimension of time, our life is a continuous path, paved with the tiles of the moments of time that all look the same. We walk on this path, always moving forward, never back, from our first moment until our last, here, on Earth. We step from tile to tile. The tile on which we stand is always the present of our life. The tile ahead of us is our future. The tile behind us, from the moment we took the second breath, is our past. We carry the time of our life always, a bag hanging on our shoulders. Human beings that we are, besides the present, usually, we carry the past in this bag, too, and worry about the future, carrying it also in this little bag of ours.

This is a kind of attachment, of which we talked in the previous paragraph.

The past can be a heavy load. Leave it behind you, truly; do not think about it. Do not brood over it; do not regret its ending: It will not change it and it will not bring it back.

Worrying about the future, and certainly after we did everything in our power to secure it, is pointless, since this will not change the outcome. For that matter, doing nothing to secure the future and then worrying about it is simply foolish.

Carrying the past and worrying about the future while being in the present, as a permanent and unchanging way of existence, means that we are attached to our projections in time, instead of taking care of ourselves in the present, only. If we take care of the present, the rest will take care of itself as a matter of course. A well tended present leads to a good future, leaving behind a pleasant past. This, of course, is true when all things are equal, because our current reincarnation cycle plan may call for other things in our life. Even so, we may smooth the corners, a little, of an otherwise rougher set of circumstances, if we are conscious of our life and plan it with wisdom and care.

Try to carry the present, only. Discard the past and the future from your shoulders; put them to rest. Do not lament the past for its wrongs, nor miss it for its rights. Do not worry about the future. Care for the present only. Do not worry for it, care for it. Do this consciously, being fully aware of it.

Every time you step from the tile you stand on, the present of your life, onto the tile ahead of you, the future of your life, take off the bag hanging on your shoulder. Put it down on the tile you stand on, the present. Do not worry about the tile ahead of you, the tile of the future; do not worry yourself with any thoughts about its content. Only when you step onto the tile of the future, take the bag that is there. Now, you are in the present. Then, the bag that you left behind you, will be your past. Forget about it. You left it there, remember? Nothing you do now, not one action, will change it one bit. Now, a new future is ahead of you. Do not worry about it; swap the **worrying** with **caring** for it by **tending** to the present. When you do this, you live in the Eternal Present.

The mere stream of time in the physical world, once it flows into the future—which for us, humans, is an unmade, yet, an unperceived and invisible world—turns the present into past. We are always in the *here* and *now* of matter. What we had done, is our past. What we shall do, will be our future. Our performed actions are behind us, always. The future is unborn, yet, and it contains our intentions, our intended actions, only.

Here and now, every second of our life, only the actions in process are with us. We can safely include our feelings and our thoughts in them. What will always be in the future are the results of our actions.

Make your life an eternal present. It brings a distinct and unmistakable sense of bliss. It widens the horizon infinitely, making it endless, from end to end. It is not fragmentized in the standard three parts of time, past, present and future.

Anchoring our life soundly in the eternal aspect of Time by living in the Eternal Present, we stand firmly on a solid and unmovable rock, unbothered by the ephemeral, lesser and lower aspect of it. Our eyes are tranquilly set on the horizon; we do not narrow our attention by focusing it on a certain object. Everything is included in the endless vista ahead of us, the landscape of our life. We live here and now, serene and untouched by our past, which we know is there, and unruffled by the future, which we know will come. We live in the *Eternal Present.*

A Lofty Point of View

It would be advantageous to have a perspective of whatever we do. It facilitates the possibility to compare things in their relative importance, observing their actual relationship to each other and to the whole. Because of the fact that in Spirituality we, actually, deal with the manner in which we conduct our life, establishing a perspective of looking at it enables us to assess the relative significance of the different aspects of our life, its different parts and occurrences, and, ultimately, the significance of it all.

To be able to see things in perspective, we have to take a distanced point of view from which we can see the whole scene in question in a panoramic vision.

From this observance point, we shall be able to see the drama of our life unfolding in front of our eyes in a detached manner, following the important prescript of Non-Attachment described above.

The drama of our life is played live on the landscape of our world every minute of it, every second, continuously, from the moment we were born. In an attached state of being, which is ordinary for an uninitiated person, the individual whose drama is played on the stage, is one of the personages in it; he is the drama itself, actually, completely identifying with it. This identification is the result of the hypnotic grip that the world, the matter in which we are deeply entrenched, holds on us.

To look at our life at play with detached eyes that are able to discern the flitting from the stable, the ephemeral from the eternal, we need to put ourselves in a point that is distanced, higher and not on the stage on which this drama is played. This place can be found only behind the scenes of this stage, in the coulisses, a place where we can keep a serene eye on it, avoiding the hustle and bustle that it creates, by keeping our Non-Attachment toward it through a detached attitude.

Positioning ourselves in this point, we see it all, we feel it all, but we do not let it take us with it, we do not involve ourselves with it beyond the immediate practical point of dealing with it. We are active, resolute and determined in everything we do; we are certain, very much assured that this is what we need to do and to accomplish. We act there consciously, fully aware of what we do, but we are not there.

We do not go anywhere with anything we do, because we do not allow it to carry us with it, we just do it, observing it detachedly, in an impersonal way, just as The Self is observing us.

We do not allow ourselves to be hypnotized by the world and by its impact on us.

The parade of our actions unfolds in front of our eyes in a constant, ever-changing procession, while we stand in this self-imposed Observation Point, coming as close as possible to The Self.

Involvement and Happiness

Throughout the last three tools, the Non-Attachment, the Eternal Present and the Point of View, there was one instruction, directive, if you will, that recurred often. You have met it before throughout the book, and you shall meet it again in various forms.

This dictum expressed the idea that everything we do, we should do consciously, being fully aware of the act of doing it. We should do it in earnest, as if it is the most important in the world at the moment. Of course, remember, we do it in the best way we can while keeping our detachedness from it, observing it from our observation point behind the stage on which the action is taking place.

This cool-headed seriousness is sheer involvement, pure and impersonal in the same time. Its purity stems from our full, conscious immersion in it; the impersonal way of doing it, stems from the detachment with which we do it.

It is, also, *happiness,* pure, simple and basic happiness.

We are happy only when we do not suffer in any way, never, anywhere. This happens when we act seriously and impersonally. Why so? Simple!

It is because whatever we do, we do so putting the whole of ourselves in it, concentrating in the effort it takes, aiming to do our best, without wanting anything, not the object itself on which we work, nor the result of this work. Our worldly ego is not there. The task at hand is the only important thing in the world right now, remember? And we observe it and our actions detachedly, remember? How can we suffer when we do not want anything, when we do not need anything? We are not anxious to accomplish something, anticipating its outcome; we just do it. We do **now** what has to be done **now;** there is no past, no future, only the present, the Eternal Present. We do not worry about the past since we did our best; we do not worry about the future, because we care for it the best we can and because we are not there, yet; what we do, we do now, so we are in the present. We are in a state of bliss, derived from the sheer impersonal, dedicated effort with which we do the task. This is happiness, and it is derived from pure impersonal involvement.

Be to the point

And while you are doing the things you do from the right point of view and being totally involved, be to the point. Do not overdo, and do not underdo doing less than needed.

Do not compare anything, lest you judge.

Say what is necessary, not more, not less. I remember my mother telling me, "Greeting is noble, son; answering it, is an obligation". She meant to say that greeting is up to the person considering it, but once you were greeted, you must answer it and in kind, so you did what was necessary.

Take and give only what is needed, do not exceed; in matters abstract and concrete, in food as in love.

When in the canteen or in the Chinese buffet, put only a reasonable quantity on your plate, so when you end your meal you do not have to throw the excess, finding yourself wasting.

Love your child or your spouse in the natural measure, do not drain yourself and spoil them with an overdose of love. You will always know how much is not too much and how much is not less than necessary, using your common sense, your inner wisdom.

Be unassuming. When you come in, no one should hear it; when you go out, no one should see it.

Do not keep a notebook, keeping count if what you did was deserved, if you will be given in return, if you will be given in kind. Do not give much thought to the extraneous circumstances of your necessary actions. Just do them when it is necessary, in the necessary manner. Be to the point.

The Quantum Qualitative Leap

"We are in this world, but not of this world"

We are a vehicle for The Self, living in this world temporarily, trying to learn our lessons, advancing on our way toward the ultimate reunification with our true ego, The Self.

Love is the ultimate glue that connects us with The Self. The duty is ours to love It with all our might, with all our heart, body and soul, unreservedly. However, since we are here, in this world, we need to do it in the proper manner.

Instead of living in this world aspiring to The Self, live in The Self while observing the world you are in" (DB)

To love wholly, the way we ought to love The Self, demands absolute dedication, total self-giving to the subject of our love. Doing such a thing demands a very peculiar state of being, one in which we are in two places in the same time. We are here in the matter, but we are required to be with all our heart, body and soul, somewhere else, with our Self, so while we are still the worldly us, we are the loved one in the same time because *we are what we are at,* right?

However, since *there is only one truth regarding one issue,* we can easily reconcile the apparent division of ourselves into two contradictory parts, by understanding that if we act according to the above dictum, our real identity, the only existing truth regarding us, is with The Self. We are here, in this world, while observing the drama of our life from the point of view of The Self.

All of the above indicates a dual nature in us, one in which we may identify ourselves with, and are, two things at the same time: *substance* and *energy, matter* and *spirit.* This particular dualistic nature is revealed to us specifically because we are on the spiritual way.

According to a very interesting theory of conventional science, the Quantum Theory in physics, this is where and what we are. Using the terminology of this theory, we are both things at the same time, presenting our two aspects simultaneously in two situations, one aspect predominating in one situation, the other in the second.

As sleeping, uninitiated individuals, we are aware only of the *matter* of which we consist; we are sure that *substance* is all there is to us. Rising from our slumber through some form of initiation, awakened to see our identity and source, we make, finally, our first steps toward it: We aspire to find The Self and to unite with it. In this case, our *material* aspect predominates: Still encased in it, and unable, yet, to set ourselves free from it, we set our eyes on high, hoping to see The Self, aiming consciously to unite with it. Standing here, we look there.

Our second, *energetic* aspect, the Spirit in us, predominates in the proactive seeker of the spiritual, the seeker who chooses to walk The Way in a "down to business", serious attitude. Such a seeker is trying actively to identify himself with The Self, and, while at it, he calmly and detachedly observes his life, the world he lives in, the realm of matter. Standing there, he looks here.

So, yes, we are in two places at the same time, but, in each of them, only one aspect has the upper hand. The proactive seeker occupies a space here, in this world, but, in fact, he is elsewhere, where the love for The Self takes him.

Enlightenment

Everyone is talking about *Enlightenment.* I heard about it ever since I started to walk The Way, and, in the beginning, I yearned for it badly in quite an attached way, which, as you know by now, is not advisable. We used to ask each other "Did you have enlightenment, already?" Hmmm..., not even asking "Did you reach enlightenment...", but "...have..." Now, I am wiser, and I know how to understand it and how to try to achieve it; I know much better what it is. I even had some rare glimpses of it, but they were there all right, I saw it, I experienced it. Everyone can see and feel it after quite a short while on The Way. You know it the moment it appears.

Enlightenment here is meant in a spiritual sense, not as a common insight into some worldly problem. It means, and is, the immediate result of being one with The Self. At this moment, the *enlightened* person understands *it all* and sees *it all,* he is *there;* he is having a firsthand experience of what it means to be reunited with The Self.

All means all that is not of this world, the transcendental existence that is there for the experiencing person to grasp.

This *all* is a nothingness exuding a real, palpable presence; it is an absence of everything, which, nevertheless, radiates a reality of fullness and a full reality.

This is a pure, uncorrupted and unadulterated occurrence that has to be experienced in order to be felt, understood and appreciated.

At this point, there is an unmistakable sense of *being at the root of it all,* in a state of utter *immobility,* completely disconnected from the worldly identity. The person is free, he is in a state of perfect bliss, and, while leaving everything behind and having none, he does not need anything because he has everything he really needs: He is with The Self. He is truly "rich" and free.

The freedom he gained is an immediate result of the disconnection from his worldly persona, and of the complete identification with The Self.

The worldly body is not there to demand its needs.

Therefore, he has no desires. Having no desires, he does not suffer.

Devoided of the misery, the agony and the torment that the worldly desires inflict upon us through the suffering they cause, we are filled with the infinite freedom given by the act of leaving the world behind. In this state, an acute perception of The All is present, together with the connective binds of the transcendent love that make it whole, in perfect alignment with The Law of Unity and its first derivative, The Law of Universal Love. This is the Enlightenment sought so hard by so many for so long.

Enlightenment stems directly from being one with The Self and consists of three things: an experience of bliss, an insight of perfect unity and an uncontested feeling of endless, unconditional and unselfish love.

This insight is the ultimate perception of the unity that characterizes the Universe with all the myriad, varied manifestations of the Creation in it, a perfectly knit whole.

The bliss sensed leads, almost naturally, to the additional intuitive and immediate understanding that the Unity prevailing in the Universe is there because of a special kind of binding: Love. This is an additional insight that accompanies the insight of Unity. It is also instantly understood that this love is the kind of love mentioned before, unconditional, unselfish and endless.

The Enlightenment that descends upon the Seeker in those rare moments provides a clear and axiomatic view of the Universe. He perceives himself as part of an entity comprised of united diverse parts, bound by love.

The truth lying at the bottom of our existence is unveiled before the eyes of the higher mind. In its self-evidence, this ultimate truth is instantly present to the higher mind, and is perceived by it immediately and completely through an intuitive "sight" of the cognized information because it does not need the intermediate lower, worldly mind to analyze and assimilate it.

Transcending the world of matter in which we live toward the unity prevailing in the Universe around us in all its manifestations; feeling as one with it in an unimpeded, absolute measure; imbued with the love that binds it all, understanding it fully without any need for an explanation, all these, combined, are Enlightenment.

Feelings

Wondrous and beautiful is the world of feelings in its amazing richness and exquisite panoramic scenery. Yes, some feelings are bad and some are good, so good that we do not let them go, and so bad that we do not let them go either.

In the context of the explanation that Spirituality offers to the theme of the human body, the feelings form a body of their own, one that is higher than the physical and less dense. More about this in Chapter Seven, section "The Structure of the Human Body" dedicated to this theme.

Feelings enrich our lives immensely and they are important in that, as mentioned, they allow us to reach the higher planes, the physical one being the lowest, and so, they help us in the process of our quest for the Spiritual, to which we are ascending.

Our actions have an impact on the world around us, and the surrounding world has its impact on us. These influences generate sensations and feelings, which, consequently, enable us to react in ways suitable to what we had just experienced and felt.

In the realm of the four Kingdoms of Creation, the Mineral, the Plant, the Animal and the Human, we find a gradual, ascending variety of feelings and reactions, from sheer absence of them, to a full basket.

A stone, a representative of the Mineral, inanimate, Kingdom of Creation, seems not to react to anything.

Plants, the manifestation of the second Kingdom of Creation, will react to positive and negative surroundings, as affections or dislikes, calm and melodious or noisy and violent music, with two extreme reactions: withering, even dying, in the case of negative ambience, or thriving and blossoming, in the case of positive environment. They will react even to feelings between the humans surrounding it. No one knows, though, if those physical reactions are accompanied by feelings, probably not, but the ambient vibrations surrounding a plant will definitely affect it. These vibrations may cause chemical reactions in the plant that, in turn, cause the plant to blossom or wither. Whatever the explanation, here, again, as in the case of stones, we are not able to know if all this is a form of feelings as we define them, because of the lack of what we know as "body language". Though plants are an organic manifestation, besides the two reactions described above, which are extreme, they cannot show by definition other reactions, and we cannot have any proof that the visible reactions represent any kind of conscious behavior.

Animals, the manifestation of the third Kingdom of Creation, will show a broader range of reactions from which we are able to understand that they have a certain array of feelings.

Years ago, I had a beautiful Dalmatian dog. Every time one of us, my wife, my kids or I, came home, he ran like crazy all over the house, jumping on the beds and the sofas. His tail wagging violently, almost popping out of his body, he was jumping on us, too, licking our face, but the most notable reaction, unbelievable for us all, at first, since we never saw such a phenomenon, was that of a recognizable smile on his face. He smiled broadly, or was it a soundless, true laugh, with laugh lines around its mouth. It was a joy to see him so happy.

So there is an ascending variety of reactions and feelings in the Kingdoms of Creation surrounding us, from the inanimate mineral, through the reacting, only, plants, to reacting and feeling animals.

We, humans, the fourth Kingdom of Creation, react to the various stimuli in a way that shows unmistakably a great variety and depth of feelings, from the extremely positive to the extremely negative, from happy and elated to sad ones. Our feelings can run the whole gamut of intensity, from the faintest to the most intense.

One of the most important features of the human feelings is the difference between the character of the feelings shown by women and men.

Academic researches on human attitude and behavior point to the fact that women, as a gender group, act from an emotional point of departure, while men, as a gender group, from an instrumental one.

This conclusion is further supported by the common knowledge, now, that the brain's two hemispheres work in two different ways which are identified with the two human genders, the feminine and the masculine, though things are not as simple and straightforward as it may sound. There is, of course, the individual predisposition in men and women to be taken in consideration, and the fact that the brain hemispheres act in some measure in an overlapping manner.

However, put in a general and schematic way, this relatively recent knowledge of the human brain states that the left hemisphere works in a technical, linear and logical mode, and that it is predominant in men, while the right hemisphere in an artistic, emotional and intuitive style, and is predominant in women.

As it appears from the analysis of the brain mode of action, women are more prone to **feel** and less **technical** than men. This important understanding of the inner workings of the world of feelings in men and women, points to a profound difference between the genders regarding spirituality, with the advantage in this regard to women. This distinction is related directly to the issue of the structure of the human body and the individual spiritual evolvement.

The human body is a package of matter and energy. In the occult circles, its structure is believed to be one of an upward scale, from matter toward energy, from denser to rarer, matter being denser than energy. The physical part of the human body is considered the densest. In the occult representation of the human body, the feeling body is the second one. It follows the physical body, upward, and is less dense.

In our quest for spirituality, we try to ascend from matter, where we presently are, to the spiritual. We ascend from the dense to the less dense on our way to The Universal Self.

Eventually, as stated before, we shall put our foot on the highest stage of the ladder, want it or not, but it will help us greatly if we make this ascent of our own volition, our own initiative. Looking at this ascent as if it were a personally initiated quest, which this book is all about, would therefore imply an important thing.

From the short presentation of the physical and the feelings bodies, it follows that the body of feelings is the one toward which we should aspire next in our self-initiated, voluntary quest.

In this light, let us see where humanity on the spiritual ladder is. More specifically, let us look at the relative place of the two genders of humanity, women and men, on this ladder.

Since the academic research shows that the women's approach to life and to the surrounding world is emotional, they seem to be already at the stage of the body of feelings, showing an obviously greater connection and synchronization with them; therefore, it appears that, spiritually, they are more evolved than men.

Through their menses and through the act of giving birth, women are more immediately and intimately in touch than men are with time and matter, as if they were more attuned to a linear and technical approach, characteristic to the brain's left hemisphere modus operandi, but the inverse is true. Women give little attention to time and instrumental systematizing of the surrounding world, compared to men. They also show an uncanny skill to *feel* things more accurately than men do, a trait characteristic to the brain's right hemisphere. Through some non-intellectual, intuitive process, they are more knowledgeable of the ongoing basic issues of life.

Women may not know how to hit a nail, but, in many instances, they will know how and where to find it and how to get it, better than men. In addition, because of this pronounced and effective presence of feelings in their mind frame, women will show a distinct skill for detecting physical and emotional needs of others and addressing them. This is what is known as Emotional Intelligence, which women are endowed with and men lack, in general.

As a rule, they will also put their needs beneath the others', more than men will. This trait of character shows in a definite way that women are capable of acts of self-sacrifice more than men are, enacting in a natural way The Law of Universal Love. It is to be emphasized that it is not that men are not doing sacrifices, but that women are more prone to, and more capable of it. Women are greatly more patient than men are and more giving and forgiving, they are also friendlier on a first encounter basis.

All these traits of character show a more spiritual approach to oneself and to another as a gender inclination, and so, I do think that women are already initiated and more advanced than men are on the spiritual way.

It appears that there is an important paradox characterizing the difference between the genders. While women are closer to matter internally, being driven to it naturally for the reasons stated above, the menses and the birth giving, they are closer to spirit than men are, by being more attuned to their feelings. Men are closer to matter externally, by being able to manipulate it more than women. However, they are attuned to their feelings definitely less than women are, a lot less, sometimes to the point of utter denial.

"Be as women!"

So said Buddha. Interestingly, in The Book of Enoch, an old Jewish apocryphal book written a few centuries after Buddha, it is stated that the knowledge has been given to women. Now those interesting statements point to the superiority of women in this regard.

Remembering that Buddha exhorted his disciples with this dictum and that Enoch had thoughts in the same vein about the subject, my statement that women are more evolved spiritually than men are that I had entertained for a long time, without knowing the above sayings of those great sages, makes much sense. And not for nothing did Buddha advise it and Enoch so said.

Women are more evolved spiritually than men. They demonstrate a kind of intelligence which men do not, one that facilitates a smoother interaction between members of a group. Men show intelligence that facilitates a smoother interaction with the environment.

This feminine intelligence is something that we, men, still have ahead of us, if we are to attain The Self, so let us, men, make our way up, toward The Self, by recognizing and embracing our feelings, and, in so doing, conquering the body of feelings through a positive assimilation, as women do it naturally, already. Let us be like women.

Awareness and Wakefulness

The state of awareness, of being aware, is an important tool in this endeavor of ours.

The point is to be aware fully of our place in this world, of our place in the spiritual development, aware of the impact of our actions on others, of our ability to forgive, to understand, to show love, true and genuine love, without being judgmental. And of course, **to be aware that we need to be aware**. This is true at all times

We tend to forget that we need to remember to be aware.

This state of mind requires an ongoing effort on our part because of the hypnotic sway the world has on us. Again, the principle of Non-Attachment helps greatly, here.

Being aware does not come easily, for to be aware, one has to be awake; one cannot be aware while sleeping.

Here, the legend about the tea plant comes to mind. It narrates that Buddha, while sitting under the famous, old banyan tree under which he had the momentous insight that led to the philosophy which bears his name, he sensed the state of "sleep" in which he was. To enable himself to be "awake" and so to escape this dreadful situation of sleep, he cut his eyelids so he could stay awake. On the place where his eyelids fell, the tea bush grew. The legend points to the fact that humanity has to wake up from its state of sleep and that Buddha's deed helped to show the source for a substance that helps us to stay awake, a prerequisite for being aware.

"Awareness exists in minerals; it sleeps in plants; it is half-awakened in animals; it is fully awakened in humans"

This maxim is a descriptive statement of the situation in which awareness exists in the four Kingdoms of Creation.

Speaking about us, humans, the statement says that in us, the awareness is fully awakened. However, I said before that we, humans, are in a state of sleep, so how are those two statements compatible?

The maxim above states that when we "sleep" in the spiritual sense of the word, the awareness is at its full potential. When we are "awake", it is activated.

Let us live up to our full potential and make good use of the awakened awareness in us, as humans. Let us wake from the slumber and activate it.

Bhikkhu

Buddha said,

"Live as Bhikkhu!"

"Bhikkhu" means monk in Hindu. Translated freely it says, "Live in this world as monks".

From him, The Enlightened, such a saying is a directive. Like the former one, "Be like women!"

To understand this directive, we have to know what a monk is.

Monks are members of a fellowship living as a closed community in a monastery. Usually, they belong to an order of monks. The order has a strict set of rules for the behavior of its members who are expected to act accordingly. All members dedicate themselves to the aims and goals of the order.

From the above short definition, it would follow that such an individual will find it difficult to live as a monk in the world at large.

The world is a wide-open place. It has laws, of course, written and unwritten, rules, norms and mores, and everyone in the community is expected to live by them. However, these laws leave within their limits some leeway of free behavior, free personal life.

In a monastery, the rules are strict and very disciplinarian, defining and regulating the lives of the monks to the minutest detail. They leave almost nothing to the fancy of the individual.

All this is a yoke that the monks take upon themselves willingly, to promote three main explicit goals.

One goal is the potential elimination of all temptations on the way of a spiritually aspiring person, so that he or she may advance, facing the fewest possible obstacles. This is why they live in a closed community consisting of one gender, only, though in the East there is, or at least was, to my best knowledge, an exception to this, too.

The other goal is to advance with a common effort the objectives of the order to which they belong.

The last goal is the provision of mutual support on the way they all walk.

Living truly and wholeheartedly in a spiritual way, demands quite much of anyone who undertakes the spiritual quest. Monks do so under extreme discipline, constantly exercising great asceticism in many domains.

This strict environment exerts great mental and physical pressure. The life in a group that dedicates itself to such goals makes the burden easier to bear.

In this regard, it is worth mentioning that there are monks who choose deliberately to live a lonely life by living as hermits, in reclusion, but free to come and go, or even in more extreme conditions, as *anchorites*. The later live in solitude in an enclosed room in a monastery, or nearby, or in some remote and lonely place, such as a cave, and an assigned monk, or some other person, tends to their daily needs. They vowed to live such a life; they are not to leave their room ever. Everything that is given to them and taken, such as food and other personal needs, is passed through an opening in the door or the wall. They are the extreme examples of such dedication.

So, when aspiring to live a spiritual life, how can a person follow Buddha's advice and live in this world of temptations as a monk, when real monks do everything in their power and exclude themselves purposefully from this world to subdue and eliminate lures from their lives?

Well, it is possible, but it requires great strength of spirit and body. It requires strong self-control, self-discipline and self-restraint.

When in this world, and we all are in this world, we face so many things that are in so many instances real temptations, threatening to disrupt our spiritual routine and self-imposed rules and measures with which we try to conduct our lives in order to attain our goal. It is hard to ignore such things and walk away, pretending that nothing happened. I say it again, however: It is possible.

Not knowing, though, how Buddha intended to implement this directive of his to be a monk in real life, applying his instruction we must remember that we are not angels, and so, no one expects us to behave angelically. Nonetheless, we **are expected** to try our best when making our way toward our goal. It is the sincere, wholehearted attempt to be an angel which is important, knowing perfectly well that while living here, there is not a chance in the world that we shall be one. This has been mentioned before in another context and is worth repeating here.

The dedication, the self-sacrifice that goes with it, the conscious and sustained effort to walk The Way and attain the goal, those are the things that matter in the end. We are not expected not to fail ever, but all the eyes are on us to see if we try truly, and our eyes first.

So be a *bhikkhu* and try your very best to be an angel

while here, in this world. Do what you do in earnest, without expecting any reward, without giving a second thought to what you achieve or not, just do it and live with Non-Attachment in the Eternal Present.

Accept the mistakes you do on the way, accept the inevitable failures, forgive yourself for them and always promise to yourself that next time you will try to do better. Fall seven, stand up seven. The same attitude is required toward the others in your life and society, always promising to yourself that next time you will forgive them if you did not this time.

Correct and Incorrect

Applying the rules and measures detailed above, brings to mind one issue, among many others, that throws a particular light on this quest.

The question that is the subject matter of this passage is what behavior would be in full accordance with the principles that we decided to follow in our quest? Putting it in another, more defined way, the question is what is right and what is wrong, what is good and what is bad, or, more abstractly, what is correct and what is incorrect?

This question has been answered before, already, in the first chapter, when we talked about The Law of Universal Love and in the relevant passage in this chapter. The answer was that everything that is in accordance with this law, would be right, however, this theme can be approached from a somewhat different angle, one that has a deep meaning for us.

The approach that I propose is one that says that there is no such thing as "good and bad", there is no such a thing as "right and wrong", and therefore there should be no such thing as "sanctions", rewarding or punitive.

Instead, what should replace those notions is the accuracy, the relevance and the appropriateness of our actions to The Law of Universal Love, their **correctness** or **incorrectness** in the light of this law. Acting in accord with these definitions, will bring us automatically in the frame of the mundane and human 'good' and 'bad' terms, but from a transcendental point of view, suitable with our quest.

The reason for this profound statement, and for what some may see as a surprising stand that may have a deep effect on social matters, is that we, as members of the very society that we try to regulate, make the rules that define our social behavior. We define the rules for our own conduct by ourselves.

This is a clear conflict of interests. Defining the rules by which one is behaving, one may succumb to the path of least resistance and find himself lenient about his own conduct, giving himself leeway in matters which will disturb him most, and freedom in matters that will please him most. Nor can one forward this fundamental societal function to another, deemed more suitable for the task of implementing it, for this other is as human as the one who gave it to him, and so, having the same strengths and weaknesses.

In order to avoid such possible conflict of interest that can lead to grave misinterpretations and alterations of truth and justice, and to ensure absolute objectivity and impersonality in defining the law, we are in an imperative need of a source that resides outside the frame of the society.

This source should be also objective and transcending the personal, immediate needs of the individuals, one that will be blind to flitting personal whims.

As stated so many times before, the human necessities and perceptions have their roots in the ephemeral matter, the realm of the world in which we live, so the *ephemeral* should be dismissed for serving as a source for such an objective and universal law.

If the world of matter in which we live is unsuitable for such a purpose, the only other possibility left for us is to look to the other available source, its opposite on the spectrum of matter—spirit upon which we and the whole universe dwell, the spiritual.

There, in this part of the spectrum, we shall find the *transcendental*. It is there from where we can draw the rules, the laws that will help us to direct **correctly** our conduct. There, we can find the objective rule of measure that does not discriminate and does not give occasional and unjustified precedence to anyone and to anything. It is there, in the transcendental end of the spectrum, that we can find The Universal Law of Conduct.

Love is the glue that holds together the Creation, the Universe. Its ability to make possible the co-existence between the various members of the Creation without infringing upon the rights of others while ensuring the individual existence makes it the best promising candidate for such a lofty task. I do not know a better alternative for this.

Holding high the flag of The Law of Universal Love as the rule that should be adopted for deciding what is the correct and incorrect way of conduct in our life under any circumstance and abiding to it will bring much progress in our endeavor to evolve spiritually. It will also bring progress to humanity as a whole, in all areas of life.

Therefore, the proper way to behave and to live is to carry out in a correct way all we do, no matter what, no matter when and no matter with whom we are involved—the way of love.

The aim should be not to do it because it is *good,* nor because we shall be *rewarded,* but because it is in accordance with The Universal Law of Love and therefore it is *correct.* Acting according to The Universal Law of Love will diminish, to the point of elimination, the natural tendency to behave in a manner that puts our own needs first without considering the needs of others, when those two bundles of needs oppose.

Doubt

On our way in this quest, there will be sometimes uncertainty and hesitation along the road, as to the aim we set for ourselves. It would be foolish to think otherwise. Only unsuspecting innocents will not give their mind, occasionally, to the possible obstacles in the project that lies ahead. The wise and the experienced have butterflies in their stomach, fearing possible failure in any project they undertake. It is only natural to have such setbacks in the determination we promised to ourselves to apply for the attainment of this goal.

It is the doubt as to what we do of which I am talking, one of the most powerful negative influences in our lives.

When in doubt we are like someone who is standing on the edge of a cliff, about to fall any second.

On the other hand, in opposition to doubt, certainty, wisely felt certainty, is one of the most powerful positive influences in our lives.

Knowing what we do, knowing where we go and to what we aim, are powerful motivators. Being unsure of all this, may sway us from our goals. Do not let doubt take over.

When present, *doubt* gnaws at our certainty and determination, wearing them away. It works so counterproductively in our projects that it is compared to Satan. While we are not engaged in a religious context, this comparison shows the negative quality attached to doubt, and the importance attributed to certainty.

The trait of self-assurance in knowing what we do, where we go and what we want has to characterize and imbue all our undertakings. Never let a hint of doubt, which will be there, of course, make the smallest dent in the certainty with which we accomplish our task. Doubt will make us lose our balance over that cliff, leading to our fall. Let us be sure at all times that what we do is what we must do. Let us have always the inner conviction that the assignment we took upon ourselves is something that we have to bring to fruition, to a good and successful end.

Applying this principle to the quest in which we are engaged, implies that we need to be on the safe side in carrying it on, the opposite side of doubt. We need to feel the assurance that this is what we ought to do. Let us not veer from the path we chose. Once we decided upon it, we should not doubt for one moment the necessity and, indeed, the personal obligation that we have to take upon ourselves this Quest for Spirituality.

Look straight ahead, hold your head high and walk on the spiritual path with a cheerful mind and a loving heart, acknowledging with determination and certainty the goal to which you aim and that in the end you will be there.

Love versus Like

Sometimes, along the way, a very specific question will nag us and disturb our peace of mind, though rightfully so.

Occasionally, we have a feeling of animosity toward someone or something and a feeling of discomfort will poke us. We ought to feel love toward the whole of creation always, so why this sentiment of disliking that we feel? It seems that in spite of the clear commandment to love all and always unconditionally, unselfishly and endlessly, we are unable to feel and show this kind of love and in the measure expected of us.

The problem is not with you. It lies in the misunderstanding and the confusion surrounding those two feelings, loving and liking.

Not to worry! There is a simple explanation for this apparent inner contradiction. It will show plainly what is happening and that there is no real contradiction between it and what should really happen. Understand it and adopt it, and all will be all right. Remember, we are still humans, not angels. We are still making our way toward being angels.

The all-important tool in Spirituality is **love**. We should not confuse, though, love with something that may give the illusion of similarity. I mean by this to say that there may be something in our approach to others, in our relationship with others, that may resemble love but that is not love, really. This "something" is **to like**.

The two, *love* and *like*, may come together and may not. Paradoxical as it may seem, one may love and dislike the object of his love, at the same time.

These two feelings, which can be very profound, sometimes, may come in their full array of combinations. One may love and dislike, as mentioned, one may love and like, he may not love what he likes, and he may not love and not like someone or something at the same time.

What defines sharply the spiritual seeker from all the others is the ability to love everyone and everything always, even when he dislikes them.

"Love always, whether you like or dislike the subject of your feelings!"
(DB)

This motto is engraved with big, bold and bright letters on the flag that the spiritual seeker holds aloft.

Yes, I may not like you, but I love you, and I always will, for the neighbor you are, for the brother you are to me as sons of the same father. I shall love you always. I bear this commandment in my heart and though I may not like always what you do and what you say, I may not like the way you look, sound, smell or feel to my touch, I shall try always to dismiss this disliking from my awareness and my behavior and keep only the love for you.

In this continuous and determined attempt to keep love in the heart and soul and to dismiss disliking, we shall employ all the applicable tools and means described above.

We shall try at all times *to be to the point*; we shall try *not to be attached* to this feeling that we do not like what we sense in the other or in the world around us. We shall try *to be aware* of the fellowship of us all, and we shall try to be a *bhikkhu* and love the other truly, in spite of what we do not like in him, *without a doubt* about the *correctness* of this approach.

We shall try all these and more, as much as we know, as much as we can, unselfishly, unconditionally and endlessly, truly as The Law of Universal Love commands.

Serenity

The world around us is bombarding us with all kinds of stimuli. The senses are being attacked, as well as the mind, continuously.

Each one of these things that touch our body and our mind acts as a trigger, prompting us to react, as a most natural thing for us to do. This, in its turn, causes a rush of impulses and thoughts in us. The whole activity of our body rises beyond the normal, even if only in a small measure.

However, we should react with a calm approach and a quiet mind in the face of all the things that our surroundings present us. Correct or incorrect situations, or to use the conventional terms of good or bad, right or wrong, joyful or sad, should be met with equanimity. Strive to react with *serenity*, without being attached to the appearance of the facts. Do not let them touch your inner core; do not let them sway you into the hypnosis of matter, subjecting you into its slavery. Keep your cool, as they say it so aptly. Equally important, be to the point, which is the *how* of it, doing always what is needed, in the necessary measure and in the proper way.

Be tranquil; keep your peace of mind no matter what is transpiring in front of your eyes; be calm, no matter what your ears hear. Be serene!

Ask, Seek, Knock!

Encouraging and fortifying in the utmost is the hope, the indestructible kind of hope, which a great teacher, Jesus the Christ, expressed in one of His dictums:

> ***"Ask, and it will be given to you; seek, and ye will find; knock, and the door will be opened to you".***
> ***Mathew 7: 7***

which is a different rendition of what Jeremiah said,

> ***"When you search for me, you will find me; if you seek me with all your heart.***
> ***(Jer. 29:13)***

In the quest for Spirituality this hope has a special place. It gives us the necessary self-assurance that we may succeed **in our lifetime**. It may not happen, but we must hope it will. As explained before, the fact that, eventually, at the end of our cycle of reincarnations we shall be reunited with The Self, is unequivocal, but this should not prevent us from trying to accomplish this goal on our own initiative **and** in our lifetime.

Do not be afraid to ask, for there is always an answer. Do not be afraid to seek, there is always the possibility that you may find. Do not be afraid to knock. Maybe someone is behind the door and he may open it for you. Do not give up; always try to attain your goal, which may be the answer to a question, finding a lost thing or a desired solution, the opening of a door or possibility of an opportunity.

The situation in which we ask, seek or knock and hope that we shall be given the desired solutions, is one in which the "no" **is already** in our hands. If we need to ask, then we do not have the answer, right? If we need to seek, then we do not have the thing for which we look, and if we need to knock, then we do not face an open door but a closed one. We are in a situation in which we lack something and now we want to fill the void, the thing that is missing; but if we just wish for it, it will not come by itself. A proactive attitude is needed in order to make it happen. Nothing is yours until you make it yours, and do so in an active, dynamic manner, with a genuine enthusiasm for it. My mother used to tell me in such cases, "Son, check the depth of the sea with your finger". She meant to say that the sea might be so shallow there that I could reach the bottom, and this is so very true. Maybe you shall reach the desired thing with as little as a simple search, you can never know. Indeed, we can never know what will be, and though we are talking about what can be extreme situations, nevertheless it is true when they say that

> ***"There are no hopeless situations; there are only people who have grown hopeless about them"***
> *Clare Booth Luce*

Therefore, always hope, always think positively, see every problem and project as something that has its solution, and remember always that if you do not pursue a proactive approach, you shall be left with an unfinished business, with a hot potato in your hand, which will not make one movement by itself to correct the situation. **You** are responsible for it if you truly want to remedy the situation. If you truly want to find the missing link, the desired answer, to go beyond that closed door, beyond the veiled curtain that is obstructing your view, **you** have to do it, for there is no one who will do it in your stead.

Hope, therefore, that a dynamic and proactive approach will bring you to the desired goal, or at least closer to it, than rather standing idle and wishing for the situation to improve by itself.

Trust

Hope shows some measure of trust in the party which is to supply the missing link. Yes, of course, we are not sure that the concerned party will fulfill our hope, but we put our trust in the possibility that it will be so.

Trust and its fulfillment show love to and from each other, because fulfilling the trust put in us shows empathy for the hoping person and his troubles. On his part, the person hoping that you shall empathize with him and fulfill his hope, shows love for you by acknowledging the brotherhood in which he feels both of you are. The brotherhood feeling that he harbors in his heart gives him the hope that he shall receive the needed help from you, at least in some measure.

> ***"Love, and you shall trust.***
> ***Trust, and you shall be able to hope"***
> (DB)

Hope that if you seek and knock, if you ask, the solution will present itself, eventually.

Judgment and Forgiveness

One of the basic tenets of spirituality is not to be judgmental. It abounds in the New Age parlance and one hears it endlessly from its adherents. To be told in such a group or community that you are judgmental, is almost as being told that your ego is as big as your car, which of course is not spiritual.

What is the meaning of this motto, really?

As children of the Creation, we all live in the same world. Moreover, this world is a world of matter, which presents endless temptations to its dwellers. It is hard for the average inhabitant of this world not to succumb to its temptations, and, in fact, it is almost impossible. Therefore, as one of the many who are subject to similar circumstances, who am I, really, to judge the other when he finds himself in situations in which I may find myself or in which I have been too, or, God forbid the height of the hypocrisy, in which I am now? We are not the judge to make this judgment! No one appointed us to this job. In fact, by definition, we cannot be judges. The judge, the only judge, is The Creator of this world, whoever or whatever He may be. We were put here, we were stationed in this world to cross it while learning from it, and we had better do it as best as we can. We are passing through the same circumstances, the same trials and the same tribulations as our neighbor is. It is not incidental that, for example, such distant people as the Jews and the Native Indians of America have the same expression for this commandment. The Jews say, "First, put yourself in his shoes". The saying is mentioned only in the context of judging another, meaning, "Pass judgment on your neighbor only when you are in the same situation as he is". For the same circumstance, the Native Indians say, "Don't judge a person until you walked a mile in his shoes". Maybe there are other peoples and cultures that use the same expression, I do not know, but the implication is clear. "Do not judge your neighbor!" is a common old aphorism that has a few deep meanings. It means that we all are the children of the same father, brothers in life, subject to the same circumstances as we make our way in this valley of death, as it is so aptly defined in the Old Testament. As we reincarnate in this place with its sole countenance of "samsara", the cycle of birth, suffering, death, and rebirth of the Hindu and Buddhist creeds, we find ourselves in the same boat with all the others around us. Therefore let us not judge, let us not put ourselves as judges above others of the same feather as us. It is inappropriate; it is beyond our true size.

Jesus, the great teacher, said,

"Judge not, and ye shall not be judged; condemn not, and ye shall not be condemned; (Luke 6:37)"

To this, He added (in the same verse, following immediately),

"forgive, and ye shall be forgiven".

Not only did He instruct the fundamental tenets of not to judge and not to condemn the other, but He also laid another brick to build a solid house for humanity: Forgiveness for the other.

Do not judge, do not condemn, for you are not the judge. The Creator is The Judge. Forgive, and you will show a higher level of character, a more advanced one. This desired trait is of much help in our way to our Self, to our Creator. It is another much-desired step in our quest.

"Be what you are?"

This much-heard New-Agean expression, which has

been fused into the daily modern parlance, already, and was made into a battle cry, almost, is of a somewhat misleading character spiritually, to put it understated.

The meaning of this New-Age dernier cri can be defined as *"Be the true person that you are!"*, and *"Reach self-accomplishment!"* This last directive is usually accompanied with the statements *"Follow your dreams!" "Make your dreams come true!"* and *"Reach for the stars!"* among others.

These are laudable instructions, no doubt, but entirely worldly in context and implications. The motto, as presented, anchors the human being and his self-fulfillment in the worldly frame.

The self-fulfilling pursuit of any human being is to be commended. Nonetheless, from a spiritual point of view, unless such a pursuit is recognized as an integral part of the Quest for our Self and, in fact, secondary to it, this instruction can be misleading, because of its purported representation as if this is all there is. In contrast, because the spiritual quest is automatic in its successful end-result of the self-accomplishment and self-knowledge by-products, it accomplishes more—it transforms the otherwise average human into a highly self-accomplished individual while achieving the ultimate end, the reunification with The Self. Let me explain.

As defined, the Quest for The Self in us is to reconnect with it, and so, finally, to come home. For us, following this goal means that its ultimate significance is that we should redefine ourselves. From human beings disconnected from their true source and redirected to a false one—to matter, which is presenting itself misappropriated as the true source—we should redefine ourselves into spiritual beings that recognize another source for life as their true one, The Universal Self. Every possible effort should be made to reach it and reconnect with it through the individual Self.

In this process of renewed identity, if we are intent and serious enough to do it, we shall involuntarily reach self-accomplishment of **any** kind. This has to be emphasized ad infinitum, simply because this task calls for a scrupulous and systematic self-knowledge introspection, which, if the voice of the inner Natural Wisdom and its instructions are heeded, leads to ultimate self-development. In the process of this quest, we investigate our physical, emotional and mental capabilities and, many times, we do so bringing them to their limits. We recognize with utmost, almost cruel honesty what we can and what we cannot do; we find the answers to the questions of how, with what and when to do it. In the spiritual quest, the call to reach for the stars and to be who we are, acquires, eventually, a completely authentic and personalized meaning.

From a spiritual point of view declaiming, "Be who you are" disconnected from the spiritual aim, leaves the interested person in a state in which he is already, one of a lower nature. Well-meaning, and naively not giving to this issue any consideration, he might well think that the present time and place are all there is and he should "be who he is" solely in this context, the worldly frame. However, as we are inclined to believe by now, or at least are willing to consider the possibility presented here, this is not the situation. We are spiritual beings entrapped in a worldly casement. The ones who recognize it and are interested in the spiritual explanation regarding life and time and place, may be willing to apply this new definition of the human existence to a relentless, sustained quest for The Self in them, for their true legacy.

To be who you are can mean many things. If you wish to engage in whatever activity that is on your mind, physical, emotional or mental, do it if you can. Jump bungee, do wild-terrain skiing, white-water rafting, hike the jungles, anything; daydream, succumb to the love of your life; solve a math problem, anything. However, there is much more to life than purely personal pursuits of worldly nature or extreme activities, thrilling as they may be.

The purpose of this passage is to show that, on the contrary, when a spiritually trained person pursues such activities, he is who he truly is and he may be able to do them even better than before the spiritual transformation or than another who is untrained spiritually. Witnesses to this are, among other available examples, the Eastern performers of the Kung-Fu, Jiu-Jitsu, Karate, etc., martial arts. Their training, which is aimed at an intensely mundane focused physical activity, involves always a conduit that is directed by a spiritual frame of mind, one to which they connect their activities and from which they act as if it were a springboard. These amazing, and literally mind-blowing performers always call The Self and rely on it to direct them in the sheer physical, almost supernatural movements and performances that they do. "It is not I acting, but The Self!" is a common thought for them, used as guide and as a means of self-motivation. In their activities, the cosmic energy known in the Eastern spiritual philosophies as "ki" or "chi" is a constant companion and ingredient.

It is true that, nowadays, many non-religious persons are trained in these arts, it being quite widespread, but even they use the original directives in some measure, which emphasizes the spiritual side of the activity. They employ rules of conduct that are rooted deeply in a spiritual point of view, such as deep connection to their most inner core, The Self, as their ultimate instructor; humbleness, compassion, proper consideration of the rival who stands before them and proper use of force according to the circumstances, never in excess.

As good as it may sound, the much drummed, nowadays, slogan *"Be what you are"* **without** bothering to define what is it that you really are, which is a true spiritual being, is pure invitation to give in to matter. It forfeits outright our spiritual legacy, our true source and home. You can hear it in every corner, from every stage, from the mouth of every performer and presenter; its mention is almost expected, it became a parroted ritual. In most instances, the promoters of this aim of worldly self-accomplishment, as much as they are committed to the well-being of humanity or so they profess, do not mention The Self and the spiritual side of life. If they mention it, as some popular writers and lecturers do, then they mix consciously two opposing views or say the obvious without giving the proper attention to the real thing.

Yes, if this is your aim in life, be what you are and develop yourself fully in whatever decent and permissible way you can but try not to forget that it is **always** secondary to the *true you*, an appendage, only, to the reconnected You with The Self.

Always remember that self-development, which leads to self-accomplishment, comes automatically with spiritual development and that usually it is faster, better, broader and deeper.

The worldly developed and accomplished individuality is something that we can do without, in the sense that it is ephemeral. This is true also in the real sense: There are plenty of individuals, nuns and monks, or hermits, who choose to live a secluded life, one that, as much as possible, is unrelated to the world in which they live.

As opposed to the ephemeral personal accomplishment,

the reconnection with The Self is the only thing that can sate us truly. It fills us with an absolute and overflowing sense of an unmistakable authentic satisfaction, stability and self-knowledge, something that nothing in this world can give and which, usually, brings better results than the worldly pursuits.

It is true that the worldly accomplishments render us abler to cope with the worldly matters, but it is to be remembered that, usually, the skills of yesterday are not suitable for the world of today, this being the ephemeral aspect of the worldly achievements. What is of substance today will not be so tomorrow, therefore, from a practical perspective, all the accomplishments we struggle so hard to achieve are like chaff in the wind. They add to the personal experience, true, but what we really need is a state of mind and body that enables us to cope instantly with whatever comes our way whenever it may happen, under any circumstance. This can be achieved best only with the aid of a spiritually directed self-knowledge, which leads to self-development, which, in turn, leads to self-accomplishment.

These personal achievements bring us in connection with our deepest roots, producing a state of the highest concentration that is conducive to an acute presence of spirit and almost an instant understanding of what confronts us, no matter its nature. The intensified concentration puts us in touch with our inner Natural Wisdom faster and more direct.

We may safely say that a fully spiritually developed individual is abler to cope with the basic demands of life than a formally educated person. The reason for this is that the more spiritually developed an individual is, the more he sees life in its entirety, grasping more and more its broader scope, while the higher the formal education, the more it fragmentizes life into specialized and professionalized segments, theorizing it mechanistically in the process.

The Self observes life and sees it from on high, able to grasp its whole vista. Looking at our surroundings with eyes of matter, we see them always from the same height, the same level and from a close range viewpoint, never from a vantage point. All we see with worldly eyes is only parts of the whole, and those parts are ephemeral by definition. Life is like a temporary journey through an ever-changing scenery, which, in order to cope with it, we need always to develop new tools and skills. The scenery changes and we need to change also, like a chameleon suiting itself to the surrounding environment.

As opposed to such a situation that for a human has a constantly renewing face, which is always confusing at its first appearance, The Self perceives it as a basic underlying character of change, one that is endowed to matter from inception, caused by its ephemeral quality. From the matter's point of view, we are in a boat floating aimlessly on the river of matter and life, able to see only our immediate surroundings, while The Self sees the whole river, from end to end and from bank to bank.

To be what we are, to follow our dreams and to try to make them true, though commendable and helpful pursuits as they are in this life, for the spiritual seeker such commandments are only tools that he uses as a prop in this journey through life. Valuable as they are, they should never be mistaken as the only worthy goals in life, nor as the best ones, but, remembering always our source and the most laudable goal of reconnecting ourselves with it, as secondary in all respects to the quest for The Self, the ultimate pursuit.

Follow your dreams and make them true, indeed, by all means, but strive to be what you really are, a child of the spirit on his way to reconnect with his Self.

Practical Means

In this context, practical means are physical actions and concrete objects, first among them meditation. They are not so many and it is hard to make a comprehensive statement explaining in conventional terms why they are necessary in the fulfillment of spiritual aims. Nevertheless, the fact is that many schools, and many seekers with much experience, consider them so. Attitudinal means, perused above, enjoy the benefit and the luxury of a detailed explanation of whatever kind and however complicated it could be sometimes. Practical means, on the other hand, are of such a nature that their justification in using them, or their rejection, cannot be explained fully and satisfactorily in a conventional manner because of the spiritual character of the affected subject. However, besides such courageously attempted explanations, there are others, scientific ones, which can support or explain spiritual things by throwing new light on them, and I shall bring such ones as far as my knowledge enables me, and in a popular manner.

For example, it is maintained that smoking is not beneficial spiritually.

The only explanation for this instruction that I could find in spiritual sources was one that states that it can damage the *ethereal* body. That smoking damages our physical body is a well-known fact. If we believe that our body consists of a well defined structure of bodies (again, this postulate will be elaborated later on, in Chapter Seven), one of which is the ethereal, then it makes sense that smoking will affect that body, also. Since this body is the energetic matrix that enables the complete human bodily structure and energizes it, it makes sense that we should refrain from doing anything counterproductive to it, such as smoking.

Let us, then, proceed with the few practical instructions with which the spiritual seeker should be equipped. Among those, we shall deal with toxic substances and then, some other advices.

Meditation

In addition to The Law of Universal Love, the other most important tool in the quest for the spiritual is *meditation*.

This is something that anyone can do. It is easy, and it can be done anywhere and at any time; it does not require any special training and devices, it is almost immediate in its results, it is far reaching in its influence and it is fun. In short, it is a perfect tool to know oneself and the world and, most important, to find The Self, which is the aim of it all. All one needs to perform it, is the desire for it.

When meditating, you just sit, trying to be quiet and let the world slip by, and there you are, one with yourself, with the world, content and full, in need for nothing else, literally. It serves as a potent and immediate cleanser for the heart and for the soul, and so, indirectly, for the body. Its immediacy is felt... well, immediately. The only thing that contradicts all this, at least initially, is the innate human inability to be still, to be quiet, for almost any length of time.

As mentioned repeatedly, since we live here, in this world, we are hypnotized by it, and until we know better, we think that this is the normal state of things. This hypnosis has a firm grip on us and stirs strongly our thoughts and feelings. We have yet to understand and accept the fact that, relative to the surrounding world, we can be in a detached state of body, mind and spirit. Once we perceive this fact and that it is better for us to be distanced from the world around us, once we are convinced that we can be in possession of the tools to do it, we are in a situation in which we can make a conscious and deliberate decision to put them in practice. As such, meditation is the best tool of them all.

Upon deciding to put it to use, it will take only a short while for the determined seeker to be in tune with it and so, to be able to be still and concentrated for longer and longer periods of time. This will lead to more restful bodies, to purer hearts and to more peaceful souls. At first, you will be able to do it for a few minutes only, and even then, it will appear as if it lasted an eternity. After a while, this duration will be longer and longer, until you will be able to sit for hours, virtually. And enjoying it, all the while. A detailed explanation will be provided in the chapters dedicated to this subject.

Toxic Substances

There are many types of drugs, classified according to different criteria. Of interest to us are the toxic substances and the hallucinogenic class of drugs. Among the toxics, we can count the caffeine, nicotine and the alcohol related substances. As such, products containing them, in all their forms, are among the things that the spiritual seeker should avoid.

All these products have a damaging influence on the ethereal body, our energetic matrix, as explained before regarding smoking. Besides this effect, they proved to have a negative influence on a certain part of the brain, which, among other things, is responsible for judgment and concentration, two important mental and behavioral faculties in life, as in spirituality.

Hallucinogenic Drugs

The title says it all. Let it be stated from the beginning that I do not approve the use of such substances in any form whatsoever, under any circumstances. I would advise everyone not to use them, ever.

Though some of them can induce, allegedly, higher, spiritual states of mind, which are exactly what the spiritual seeker wants, they are not to be used for a few reasons.

Before elaborating on that, allow me to mention that there is a certain type of person, having what is known as "addictive personality", who is prone to be caught into the use of drugs, without hope to get out of it, or having much difficulty trying to do so. Usually, one does not know beforehand what type of personality he is in this regard, and it is not advisable to find out.

Let us, now, see the reasons for not using drugs.

One is that drugs can be damaging to the extreme. The facts are well too known, so there is no need to explain them here. I will repeat, though, my advice not to use them, as a direct and personal appeal. To this, I would add, also, a piece of information regarding the damage that drugs induce. Of late, it is known that drug use cause shrinkage of the *amygdala*, a small part of the brain, which plays an important role in motivation and emotional behavior.

The second reason is that while being in such states of mind in which we find ourselves when meditating, or in a state of high concentration, the brain and the body produce calming substances; also, spiritual and meditative states of mind stimulate a part of the brain that produces religious and spiritual experiences. Incidentally, this part of the brain is of assistance for the orgasmic sexual pleasure, so, here, we may find an explanation for the sense of bliss that we experience in such states of mind, a feeling that some, and I among them, would say that is, or can be, akin to the orgasmic sensation. There is no real need, therefore, to rely on artificial, external means for it.

Furthermore, I do not think that it is wise to bring oneself artificially to higher and more profound states of mind or awareness conditions through such means, for the following reasons.

To begin with, in the broad spiritual community, in direct contradiction to the Left-hand path, or Black Magic, adepts of the Right-hand Path, or the White Brotherhood, as it is sometime called, will not use, as a rule, external and artificial means to advance on The Way, or to attain any goal, related to it or not. Such true adepts do not **want** anything; they try to live in a state of non-attachment, in which desire is eliminated. They know that, eventually, this advancement will come, wanting it or not. Though they recognize the need for it and act proactively for its achievement, making every effort in their ability to attain it, they do not **wish** it. Everything has to come and to appear in its own suitable time, fitting the personal development as achieved through **non-attaching** efforts and means, and through personal, not external ones.

Second, an experienced seeker reaches such states of mind from the first seconds of the meditating session or even when in a profound concentration state, because he is already conditioned into them. Doing it for a long time and knowing every trick of it, for such a person it is like a conditioned reflex to reach them.

I do believe in self-sufficiency in every aspect of life, which in this case amounts to making every effort to reach higher and more profound states of mind and to attain the reunification with The Self through means that are available to us from our own sources, not external ones. On the way to The Self say no to drugs of any kind, and say yes to a genuine personal effort, which, in any case, is self-rewarding to the extent that it produces automatically the result sought for.

Vegetarianism

The practice of Vegetarianism is accepted among many Seekers. It is almost taken for granted that a spiritual seeker is a vegetarian or should be. This is not always the case, though. One of the most prominent occultists and spiritual persons of the 19th century, and, in fact, of all times, Ms. H.P. Blavatsky, the founder of the Theosophical Society, was not vegetarian. Nevertheless, she was regarded by many, and still is, as one of the most important and influential spiritual figures of our times, a luminary in her own right.

As mentioned quite a few times before, the essential point here is that the *tool* is not as important as the *intention* and the *drive* to bring it to full realization. While this is true and significant, still, vegetarianism is one of the useful tools to use, if one is able to stick to it.

The practice is old. It appeared in full with the advent of

Buddhism, which makes it c. 2500 years old, but, for example, it is known that the Chinese practiced it before that.

Vegetarianism has quite a few different and distinct forms of practicing that will not be detailed here, but, as a general practice, it does have its reasoned explanations and merits.

One, and the main of three reasons for not eating meat, is that in order to eat it, one has to kill. Some cultures, religions and religious sects, Buddhism prominent among them, prohibit killing following the commandment not to cause harm to another creature, in the same vein that one would not wish any harm to be done to him by another. Causing harm to a living creature is perceived as a negative action, an act of cruelty, selfishness and utter lack of basic consideration for others.

When killing for the fulfillment of a bare necessity of life, such as eating for the sustainment of the physical body, the act is regarded as a necessary evil. As such, to illustrate, hunters of primitive tribes ask the soul of the killed animal to forgive them for killing it.

Another reason, is the reincarnation principle in Buddhism and elsewhere. The principle says that a human can reincarnate in an animal, so it would be natural among its adherents to refrain from eating it as good measure. This practice spread with the dissemination of Buddhism and so, it is now a distinct part of the Buddhist observance and culture.

The other, third and last reason for practicing vegetarianism, is that when an animal is killed, it is filled with negative vibrations resulting from the fear and pain that accompany the slaughter.

My first instructor in spirituality presented this argument to me, and though I have never heard it from any other source since then, to me it makes much sense.

These vibrations may find their way into our awareness and soul; therefore, killing for consuming is not advisable and to be avoided.

Analyzing the above arguments, it seems that there are no real reasons for practicing vegetarianism, except for the commandment not to kill.

Bad vibes can be fought back and eradicated through the constant nurturing of good vibes and other means.

The argument of reincarnation in an animal, is not an option for humans, as far as my knowledge and logic takes it. All of the Creation is on its way forward, to its source, not backward, even temporarily, so, in my opinion, the notion and the possibility of reincarnating into an animal are fallacies.

The real problem is the killing involved in the need for satisfying an existential need of ours. The commandment says simply, "Thou shall not kill!" without much ado: Do not kill and that is that. All of the Creation is a big brotherhood, unified in essence, so do not kill. If we follow this very basic commandment strictly and unswervingly, then we made a big step toward attaining our goal, The Self.

As a tool to be employed on this quest, vegetarianism is potent because of its influence in cultivating compassion for the rest of the Creation, as well as because of the self-restraining and disciplining influence it creates in us.

If you can, by all means, be a vegetarian in one of its forms.

Prayers, Invocations and Affirmations

Though this is not a religious book in any way, allow me, please, to touch upon the subject of personal appeals to a higher authority, in our case, the highest, The Universal Self.

The title could have been presented in a different order, with the word prayer at the end of it or in the middle, in a random mix. I chose otherwise because, in my opinion, the other two represent two lower derivatives of prayer, more so the invocations. Whole books can be written about each one of them.

I touch upon this subject because prayer has a specific place in religious rites. It had rightfully earned this place because of its profound spiritual meaning, one that will be understood later on.

For the spiritual seeker, it will be helpful to know what it actually is and how to do it because it touches on higher or more sophisticated states of mind and because it involves states of high concentration.

The subject in question is the inclination we, humans, have, to approach entities higher than us when we feel that the human strength and ability, ours or those of another's, are not enough to bring the desired results. Those entities are transcendental, and are higher in terms of authority and power, of intelligence and understanding, and we feel that it is there where the ability to perform rests.

In the following passage, I refer to prayers in which we ask for help, not prayers in which we give thanks, though prayers of gratitude are necessary to establish the correct relationship between the higher authority and us.

Prayer is one of the most potent forms of asserting one's own presence and goal before the Universal Self in a humble and unassuming way.

In doing so, let us, first, define and understand the differences between the three notions mentioned in the title of the section. As prayer is the conventional form of self-expression toward the higher authority, let us begin with it.

Old as we are is the prayer. It was born with us. Entreaty, plea, application, petition, request, all these, and more, are prayers, really. We, humans, address it to God, whether it is the god in whom the great three monotheistic religions—Judaism, Christianity and Islam believe or the gods of polytheistic societies, or to the individual souls of any object in nature to which animistic societies direct their pleas.

I shall not elaborate on the above-mentioned definitions of prayer, since their meaning and implication are obvious. What is not so obvious is **how** should one pray, and **what** it does to the soul, to the heart of the praying person. What we believe will be God's attitude toward our prayer, is another important thing.

In the subject of **how** should one pray, *attitude* and *technique* are important.

The attitude to be adopted should be one of innocence and reverence. Pure and right type of concentration are the techniques to be employed.

Let us begin with the correct type of attitude. The prayer should come from the innermost recesses of our being. Our supplication should be addressed from the core of our being, from the most innocent, and untouched by the world, part of ours;

"Be as children"

said so aptly Jesus, the great teacher. Clean we should come before what we believe is our maker. Believing so, that He is our maker, we put our trust in Him and so, we pray to Him.

Reverence is the prerequisite when an individual would put his petition at the feet of a worldly authority. If such is our attitude toward a worldly authority, how much more so it should be, and indeed is, with The Supreme? Our soul should be filled with veneration for Him **well before**, not when or after, we challenge ourselves with the task of presenting our plea to Him, for it is us, not He, who are challenged when praying to Him.

The challenge stems from our recognition of the inherent, basic weakness of ours as human beings. The bare fact is that we are not omnipotent, while He **is**. We are so not only in the domain of making, of creating, and not only in the domain of changing things, but also in accepting ourselves as we are and in accepting the way in which the world around us affects us. The mere recognition of His authority confirms this basic, permanent condition of ours, when praying to Him. We would not appeal to Him if we were able to put our things in order **without** His guidance and help.

The petition we forward to Him should be filled with our whole being, our whole essence and raison d'etre. Our prayer is us and we address this whole package to Him—we and the prayer are one.

The purest and strongest concentrated identification with our bodily abilities and mind faculties should be put into this prayer, no less—when we put our prayer at His feet, we are there as well. An amalgam of hopes, feelings, wishes and problems, our whole life is presented at His feet, filtered through the prism of the problem we have at the time and molded into the shape of a prayer. We focus on this act and moment and concentrate our whole life in it. We are there with our prayer as a concerned human being seeking help for his plight, for his plans, but here is the secret of it and the type of relationship that He and we have:

"God's help is His guidance"
(DB)

God does not help. He will not interfere in the plan of our life because doing so would be tantamount to an interference in the plan of the Universe itself after it had been conceived, and this is not to be done. (This statement is one of the most fundamental issues in comprehending how the Universe operates. It touches upon the question of whether there is a *deterministic* type of operation at work or a *fatalistic* one, which is an extreme type of *determinism*. The interested reader will consult an encyclopedia or other related literature; the reading will prove to be interesting).

He, as The Universal Self, watches us through the personal Self in each of us, impersonally and without taking any part in it. He knows exactly what we are going to do in our next move, as He knows in advance every move of ours, but he will not interfere in any way. From this, it is self-understood that we cannot expect to have His help. What we can expect with the utmost certainty, though, is His guidance.

God, The Universal Self, which has The personal Self as His representative in every one of us, instructs, guides. The guidance offered is the necessary one to accomplish our part in the Grand Plan of the Universe. His absolute infinite wisdom pours incessantly into our worldly consciousness. It is always there for us, and in a form that we can understand, distil and assimilate. All we have to do is to listen and to be open to it.

Guidance and instructions are the best help in any circumstance. Even when it seems that direct, genuine help is needed, and that we get it from Him upon praying for it, it is His guidance we receive, not His help. His guidance gives us the necessary physical and spiritual strengths and the wisdom to perform the task; it gives us the intuition to approach the necessary means to advance our cause and to attract them. In the great scheme of the Universe, no task is given without the necessary ability to perform it. It would be a total waste of time and energy by Him not to do so. Therefore, one needs not to worry.

> ***"Be as the lilies of the field!"*** (paraphrase on NT, Mt., 6:28, DB)

Go for it! Do it without the least assurance that the task will be accomplished; do it beyond the necessary plans to achieve the ends, because the necessary personal and external tools needed for the accomplishment of the task are there. Just listen and be open to the Divine guidance. It is always there. For us. Pray not for help, for it is not needed. Pray for guidance, for instructions how to reach what seems to you to be His help. God is teaching us the musical notes and how to play the tune with the instruments in our hands—our life and us. Now, we can read the music and play it, the music of our lives.

The answer will come, eventually, in the form of a good advice or a timely instruction, a suddenly clearer perception of the problem, of the circumstances surrounding it and of your own abilities to solve it. It may come, also, in the form of a most providential circumstance, though coincidence it will be **not**, for this providential happenstance was there in the scheme of things, in the great plan of things, of the Universe, from the beginning of time. It had just waited for the set moment, which was about to come, to materialize itself. Therefore, it is not help, but a tool to use, put in our hands for the advancement of His plan.

Having covered the attitudinal aspect of prayer, we have come, now, to the subject of the technique of praying.

One may pray in the simplest manner: "Dear God, I have a problem, please help me, oops, please guide me!" and he may do so in the most unpretentious manner, without any acquired, premeditated technique. God will listen anyway; you may rest assured of this, because you are addressing your Higher Self, the Self in you, which is the representative of the Universal Self.

One can do it, also, in a more refined manner, more developed.

In its simpler form, the prayer is sent to God, the addressee, on the wings of your hope, with the prayer at the source of it, at its roots. The focus is on you and your prayer and on the hope that it will be answered positively.

In the more developed form, you talk with God, you have a conversation with Him, you communicate with Him directly, in a unified field of awareness. He and you are one, talking, discussing the matter, looking into each other, you in His meaning and essence and He in your eyes. The prayer is no longer a prayer; it takes the form of a very clarified and defined presentation of the problem that preoccupies you. You are not here to whine in your praying, really, because this will not help and you know that. You pray for an educated advice and one that is to the point and will instruct you in the correct way of solving your problem. You pray to get the proper instructions and guidance to find the necessary strength of body, mind and spirit to solve it, the wisdom to apply it correctly and so, to carry it out successfully. Let us see how we do it.

To put the subject in its correct context, from now on, in the light of the previous explanation, let us name prayer by a more suitable apellation. Let us choose, from among its many synonyms mentioned in the beginning of the section, the word *petition*.

Petitioning The Supreme One is a profound act. We need to concentrate fully in it, laying aside everything that does not concern it. We do so in the same way in which we concentrate on the solution of a worldly problem, to the point of oblivion to what is around us, but this time not only on the problem and on its forwarding, but also on its whole set, the personages, the problem at hand and its solution.

The set is comprised of the petitioning person, the addressee, which is God, The Supreme One, the problem that prompted us to appeal to Him and the guidance we hope to receive to solve it. This set is a communion of God and the human temple in which He resides; a communion assembled for the expressed purpose of solving a problem that the human being is confronting.

The technique that I am about to detail is fully applicable to the art of meditation, also.

The key prerequisites for the proper prayer—innocence, reverence and concentration, should be maintained in full.

Pure and clean in our thoughts and heart, knowing to whom we talk and being fully aware of it at all times, concentrated in presenting a well-defined problem in a clear manner and in directing it to Him, are the proper tools to conduct the petitioning act. All this is done by a simple act of focusing our attention properly.

When petitioning, our posture is, so naturally, one of imploring: our palms are held together, perpendicular to our chest, fingers toward our chin, or in front of us, to the side of the body, slightly bent, palms facing upward. Our eyes closed, usually, we recite our petition in our heart, in silence.

Let us look a little bit closer at all those actions that we perform instinctively, almost, when we pray, and examine them.

Our hands are spread, or held together, in a motion of

asking humbly, begging, "Please, hear me, notice me, listen to what I have to say and guide me in the situation in which I find myself!" This is how we would ask anyone to the same effect. Reverence, sincere and deep respect for the one we ask to guide us, are the keywords here. If this is how we approach a human being, then it should be many, countless times over, when approaching God. We do not know any other way to do it, so we appeal to God in our time of trial, of sorrow, in the same way.

We close our eyes to be farther away as possible from the outside world, closer to ourselves, to immerse ourselves into our inner world. We do so to be able to concentrate in this prayer of ours and to direct it to God.

The focus of our attention is the place in our head where many believe that the *third eye* is located. This place is regarded by many to be behind the middle of the forehead and above the nose bridge, and between the temples, but it really is the center of the head (read, please, the material on 'third eye' in Chapter Seven). When we close our eyes, they "look" directly at the bridge of our nose. You can focus there and concentrate while "being" in this place. But you can do better. You can make the place a stereoscopic landscape, helping you better in your effort to concentrate in your prayer, and, temporarily, to obstruct the outside world from taking front stage place and central import.

Focusing our attention properly involves a technique that is quite similar to the one applied for the viewing of three-dimensional pictures with unaided eyes. As said, upon closing your eyes, they focus automatically on the nose bridge. Try to "look" farther away from the nose bridge point **into** the field of vision ahead of you. This will make you "look" at a distance of a few inches away, up to somewhat less than a foot at the most. Looking into that field, "see" it and notice it as if it is a new world, a material universe in itself, one that can be visible with closed eyes. Shortly after doing so, almost immediately, there will come a moment when this inner world will be perceived as three-dimensional, having a stereoscopic quality to it, similar to the landscapes viewed in the external world. "See" it, do not only look at it. You will sense a slight upward movement of the eyes upon being there in the field of that inner landscape, as if bringing them into the awareness of "seeing" it by aligning them. What we do, and what happens, is like a three-way movement of the eyes, one after the other: first, closing them; second, moving them away into the field ahead of you; third, looking at the inner landscape that is there and "seeing" it.

Being there, in this inner field of vision, we are drawn immediately into it, because it functions as an authentic world, in a similar way in which the real world is functioning. This effect is a direct result of focusing our attention deliberately there.

Another and immediate result of this alternative, inner world that we made, which, in fact, was prepared premeditatedly, is that we can concentrate on it and so we are able to put aside the other world, the one in which we really live.

Putting it aside, we extricate ourselves from its hypnotic influence, if only temporarily. The real world is perceived humming softly not far away, as if it is nearby, in a valley below, while our inner world had absorbed us completely, appearing to us as **The real world**. We substituted the real world with the inner.

In this situation, something interesting happens: We are almost surprised of being fully aware of **ourselves,** in a way that leads us to observe that we forgot entirely our existential entity, we forgot ourselves, and now, suddenly, we remembered it. We suddenly recognize that we forgot to remember ourselves and now, we do.

Now, we are in a state of profound calmness and we can concentrate and dedicate ourselves to the task, to our prayer, our petition to God.

Our missive to God has to be very clear, very well defined. We have to think hard and long before we present our petition to Him. It has to state clearly what is our problem, in what situation this problem puts us and that we ask for His guidance.

When you present your petition, call Him by whatever name you wish, "Dear God", "Universal Self", "Our father in heaven", "God", "Father", it does not matter, just call Him and tell Him what is it that bothers you. Tell Him how bad you feel, tell Him in what an awkward or perilous situation you are and then ask Him for His guidance. Not help but guidance, and guidance will be given. You shall see it with your mind as a revelation, how it comes, how it appears, an utter and sudden clarification of the problem you had and of the way to solve it. It may come when you think of it with clear, lucid mind and it may come unexpectedly, right in the middle of something that you do, or while staring absent-mindedly at a leaf blown in the wind. Come it will, when you pray or later.

This short study of what prayer is enables us to understand also that it has a deep spiritual meaning. Seeing ourselves as the temple in which God resides and Him as The Universal Self, and the prayer as an act of petitioning, then when some say, "I pray to God", others may say with equal fervency of belief that they approach The Universal Self with their problems, asking for guidance.

From this, it can be understood that a line of direct communication has been opened between our worldly entity and that of The Universal Self, represented by The Self in us. This line has been there always, unbeknownst to the most of us, but now, knowing better, we opened it. No less important is the fact that there is no need for any intermediary between The Universal Self and us. The road to It is always available, all we have to do is to open it and then, we may present our problems to It at any time we wish, knowing with absolute certainty that It will always listen to them and that they will be answered always with a supremely intelligent guidance.

After this analysis and acquaintance with what is prayer, its nature and techniques, let us have a glimpse of what it does to the soul of the praying individual, to his heart and body, for it does something, no doubt about that. Now, we shall use the more general word *prayer* not only as *petitioning* but, for the ones who do so, as *praise* also.

Prayer is soothing; prayer is a calming balm spread on the soul, tranquilizing and strengthening its tormented realms, otherwise left on their own, leaving us in a quandary. Praying is the remedy we need sometimes when all else seems to fail us. It is the query with the response in it, it is the petition that is always heeded and answered; it is the praise to God as an ultimate act of recognition of the supreme governing power in our lives and of expressing our submission to Him, as in "Yours will be done!"

In the act of petitioning, the absolute assurance that we shall receive the needed guidance for the solution of our problem, for the accomplishment of our task, **without** renouncing our responsibilities, lifts a burden from our shoulders. It is telling us that we are not alone; He is with us always, everywhere when we need His guidance, and I find myself in the need of repeating that He may be God for some and The Universal Self for others. The knowledge that the supreme wisdom is offering, removes any doubt from our mind. It gives us certainty that in spite of many and difficult problems, as it may be the case sometimes, we shall have the solution for them; it gives us determination to pursue the struggle until the satisfactory result appears.

Prayer, in every sense of it, is purifying, it cleanses our inner world of the burdening residues of the outer. After praying, we feel lighter, elated, relieved of a pressing burden and, indeed, as if we fulfilled our duty to ourselves, to the Universe.

To pray is to have confidence in ourselves and in the presence in our lives of The Self, or of God—however you prefer to call this supreme sublime entity—and in its supreme wisdom and beneficial influence. Pray—appeal and listen to the voice of wisdom directing you in the right direction; praise and recognize the Self in you.

Let us turn our attention, now, to invocations and affirmations.

Invocations have the meaning of prayer, however, they have an additional meaning; it is this meaning that I intend to discuss.

Invocations are used sometimes to summon for help a higher entity or a spirit, specifically an evil one. Besides being similar to a soul, something with which we do not deal in this passage, a spirit refers to the immaterial substance – in the sense that our world is perceived as being material – of a worldly entity or a supernatural entity altogether. It may be a deceased soul, a ghost, or it may be a demon. However, when an invocation is performed, it is usually addressed to an evil spirit asking for its active help and intercession.

As deemed from the previous pages, I encourage spiritual work and engage in it on the side of the positive and the godly, not on the side of the evil and the ungodly. In my book, invocations are in the same class as toxic substances and hallucinatory drugs – not to be used. We shall touch more upon this subject in a short while.

Affirmations constitute a class of their own. The practice asserts one's power to change the inner and outer, abstract and concrete circumstances of one's life, through thoughts, specifically positive thoughts.

This kind of optimistic approach to the goal of the attainment of worldly goals in all aspects of one's life is used in the hope of changing the present situation of one's health and prosperity to the better and so, one is able, presumably, to attain well-being, wealth and power.

This line of thought, initiated in the 1890s in America, is in use by many in the broad New Age movement without even knowing that this is an existing thriving philosophical movement, namely the International New Thought Alliance. It is imbedded with some religious, even mystical and occult implications. There are, also, some other religious and occult organizations affiliated to it.

Specifically, this approach states that the application of the power of thoughts through positive and constructive affirmations in the pursuit of changing the daily life's circumstances has immediate and palpable results. As such, affirmations are said to be powerful in two types of affairs.

They are certainly powerful in the process of healing – when healing does occur in the predetermined course of things in the deterministic Cosmos, I hasten to add. It quickens the speed of the healing and fortifies the ill person beyond the conventional medical methods applied. They can be significant in improving temporarily the health of an ill person in his predetermined course of life – again, in the deterministic sense, and so, easing the suffering for a while in some measure (more about the deterministic aspect of this subject, shortly below). Many conventional academic researches confirm these improvements, both permanent and temporary, though the verdict on this is inconclusive.

Affirmations are powerful also in the difficult process of accepting hardships in one's life. Besides healing, this is maybe the most powerful and significant importance of affirmations—the ability and the strength to accept hardships without losing hope for an improvement or even for the best. "Accepting hardships" is not meant here as a passive and resigning action adopted by us submissively. It is meant as a dynamic and rather constructive approach, one in which those hardships are perceived as pieces of reality, albeit unfortunate ones, which present themselves into our life as fragments of the world surrounding us. They are a part of our life, just as the good fragments: When good pieces of life come our way, we embrace them, we laugh because of them, we remember them for the better. However, although we shall not laugh at the bad pieces of reality in our life, though maybe laughing at them will help more than we can reckon, let us embrace and recognize them for what they are: a part of our life, although an undesired one. There is a saying, affirming that

"If it doesn't kill you, it makes you stronger"

This is so true. If we could muster the inner strength and the courage to accept the difficulty in the way described above, which, admittedly, is never an easy thing to do, we could accept it as a part of our life. We can do so by not denying it and by not pretending that it does not exist. It would be better to look straight in its face and admit that this is a reality and that, want it or not, it is an integral part of our life and it will not go away, no matter how much we want it. Then, we should be able to deal with it dynamically and constructively, taking the initiative in our hands. Acting in this manner, we can turn the difficulty into a stepping-stone with the help of which we can get out of the impasse in which we found ourselves.

While I do not deny the principle behind this approach, I have two kinds of difficulties with it in trying to adopt, eventually, this philosophy.

The first difficulty is that since I believe that our fate is sealed in a deterministic fashion from the moment of our birth, indeed from the moment of our inception as an incarnate soul in this world and throughout the whole cycle of reincarnation until its end, the notion that affirmations can be used to change the circumstances of life raises some troublesome questions.

Although there is no doubt in my mind that thoughts are powerful tools, it is also my opinion that their power is limited to the predetermined and predefined frame of Creation as a deterministic realm.

From this, it can be inferred that nothing beyond the predetermined frame of circumstances is meant to be, and that the perceived power of affirmations is limited by the predetermined. The question arises, then: If the course of things is predetermined, then why taking the trouble to try to change it? And if we can change it, was this change not predetermined also?

Indeed, in the deterministic cosmos, what we see as change was predetermined, therefore it was not a change, so the affirmation had no influence at all on the ultimate course of things. But, and this the answer to the question of why trying to enact a change, we, as human beings, cannot know our fate. We do not know if it is for better or for worse. Here comes to play an important aspect of affirmations, their empowering influence: It may well be that hope, implied in the very act of making an affirmation, is warranted because the change was predetermined for the specific person, and hope is always a good addition, therefore, worthy of use, and this would be a serious consideration to make.

Entertaining thoughts of hope is an excellent weapon. It is good for a faster recovery during illness and against defeatism, against despair and disappointment, all of which can weaken appreciably our body and our immune system and the ability to accept hardships into our life without surrendering to them, without giving up right from the very beginning. Hope strengthen and fortifies, it opens new horizons and puts a smile on our face. It is always better to smile than to be grumpy, always better to hope than to despair, therefore, let us always hope. Hope is encouraging. In hoping, we recognize that the bad situation, the "no", is what we have at the moment, and what is left is the possibility that the "yes" will appear somehow. Now, wouldn't that be wonderful? If it was predetermined that we should prevail, then hope and positive thoughts only put us in a brighter spot from which we can cope with the problem better; if it was predetermined that we should not prevail, then, sometimes, hope and positive thoughts can improve the situation, albeit temporarily, and this is preferable to a constantly bad situation. If only for this alone we made the affirmation, then it was good, it was excellent: Let us diminish the suffering as much as possible.

However, I am not of the opinion that affirmations will change the situation radically, in the opposite of what was predetermined. They have a positive, encouraging aspect, which can be put to good use. To my support, I call the old art and science of Astrology. It is my belief that what the stars say, will come to be. It is not for us to change it, if we so wish, for we cannot do it. Because this book is not the place to deal with those Astrological concepts, I shall leave my statement at that, with the faith that the interested reader will follow the subject further, if he so wishes.

The other difficulty that I see is that affirmations are in contradiction with the principle of Non-Attachment. It is the implied "personal wish" in the affirmation, the *desire* expressed by it, which is in contradiction with the attitude of Non-Attachment.

In principle, as spiritual seekers, we ought not to "wish" anything; we ought not to "want" anything. *Wanting* or *desiring* as a purposeful pursuit, are an immediate and potent obstacle in our development on the Spiritual way. It stops it, or delays it in the very least.

Technically, in the most basic and purest spiritual principle, without taking into consideration any worldly aspect, anything that comes our way, the "correct" and the "incorrect", is to be accepted in our life as the right thing to be and which came at the right time and in the right measure. Therefore, we should not wish to change it in any way. This is what was meant to be. The old saying "God gives and God takes", which religious people say when someone passes away, represents this principle in the most wonderful manner, directly and profoundly.

Desire, as explained at length before, is a basic human process, one that is natural to people who are still asleep, spiritually. It has a built-in consequential mechanism explained, immediately below, as the *karma* principle.

The *Desire* derives from the fact that we live in this world of matter. It implies *Will*, a prerequisite to fulfill our desires. *Will*, in turn, means *Action*, for we act according to our *Will*. *Action* in turn produces *Karma*, "bad" or "good", as the circumstances define.

Karma is an important and fundamental notion in the Eastern religions and beliefs of Hinduism and Buddhism. It is a cosmic impersonal and natural moral law of *action and reaction*. Its concept is as follows:

"As we sow, so shall we reap!"

So goes this universal saying, and it is true. As we act, so shall we pay or be paid in return.

In the wholeness of Creation, any action, physical or

mental performed by anyone, anywhere, any time, causes a suitable reaction to it. This means that not only actions create responsibilities in their wake, but thoughts also. In the Universe, there cannot be action without an appropriate reaction, for if it were so, there would be an imbalance in the great scheme of it. This is known in the field of physics in the conventional science as "The law of action and reaction".

The Creation cannot suffer imbalance, it being an unnatural state of things. It is like tottering on one foot, and only when we put the other foot on the ground are we able to stand firmly, removing the possibility of falling. Therefore, likewise, in order to reinstate constantly the required balance, Creation puts the other foot on the ground: It causes a reaction to our action, unequivocally. The reactions to our deeds are the debts and the responsibilities left in their trail, and the rewards incurred.

Karma is the law that Creation deemed necessary to restore the balance. This law makes anyone fulfill those responsibilities, pay the debts and receive the rewards. To do so, further lives on this worldly plain of mater are required, because, usually, not all our physical and mental actions are balanced in the current life and sometimes they are not balanced fully. This is the immediate practical reason for the *reincarnation* principle, besides the explanations for the subject brought in the first chapter.

Unfinished businesses in a current life have to be finished here, in this world, but usually in a future, additional life into which we are reborn for this specific reason. Only when we cease to *desire*, the consequent necessary *will* to have it fulfilled will disappear, and so, the *action* required will be unnecessary. Without *action*, there is no *reaction*, because there will be no debts and responsibilities left and no rewards to receive as *unfinished businesses*. Without *unfinished businesses*, there is no need for *further lives* and so there is no need to *reincarnate*. Seekers who evolved spiritually to such a degree, do not reincarnate anymore and so, they are liberated from the wheel of birth and rebirth, an ultimate and momentous achievement.

In the light of the above, affirmations are counterproductive in our spiritual quest in their aspect of attachment, in the sense that they may delay our liberation from the reincarnation cycle of life and death to which we are subjected from the very beginning of our course on this worldly plane. The acquisition of the object of wanting, of desire or of lust, which is inherent in making an affirmation, is a further obstacle on our way to Self and freedom. I remind you of the discussion about possessions, in the first chapter.

There will arise, of course, the question of what to do when we encounter misfortune in the form of bad health, or plain bad luck? Should we not do our best to avert this situation, or at least to improve it? And, if affirmations help, then what, are we to discard them just because they are an impediment to our evolution on the spiritual way?

The immediate answer is that, yes, we should discard affirmations because of the imminent failure of our quest due to the incurred attachment to the issue at hand and to the results expected and produced when making them. This, in its turn, is producing *karma* automatically and imminently and with it the need for reincarnation.

However, there is another approach, which one may employ. It is the Karma Yoga system of dealing with life in a true and classic spiritual way. Also known as Kriya Yoga, this kind of spiritual approach states that, though living a worldly and active life, every action we do should be performed as an action of inner sacrifice that detaches ourselves from our doings. The action is performed not as something that is framed around ourselves as its center, intended to render a reward for us, or ending in an anticipated complete and immediate satisfaction of our cravings and desires, but as something that transcends our ego, going forward beyond it. This type of Yoga brushes aside the aversion for outright actions in life, as suggested by implication in another kind of yoga, Jnana Yoga.

In Karma Yoga, we do whatever is appropriate according to the circumstances, without thinking of our subjective and personal place in it. This means that we are objective, impersonal and unattached. We take the risk, so to speak, of *doing*, of *acting*, but without accumulating any karma, "good" or "bad". We consider our actions as necessary and do not wait nor look for the result, and do not expect any reward of any kind as an outcome – this attitude is the sacrifice involved, therefore, we are detached from the action, so it does not bind us in the eternal wheel of action and reaction. An action performed in the Karma Yoga spirit, annuls the need to reinstate the cosmic balance.

In conclusion, it will be worth to recapitulate and mention that thoughts are powerful entities and that we can certainly apply them to the purpose of encouragement in negative circumstances of our life, whether of health, fortune or spiritual well being. However, if the principle of Non-Attachment is valued in its proper context, that is, as an efficient and necessary tool in the progress on our spiritual way, and if affirmations are viewed in the light of the Karmatic principles, then they are to be viewed within the limits to which I drew attention in the discussion above.

Panoramic View and Hearing

The *panoramic view* is a very useful tool in grasping the world in all its fullness with constant immediacy and freshness and with an unconditioned state of mind. It is useful also in providing us a true perception of the real place we hold in this world, a place brought to its right proportions, one which is not bigger than us, belittling us, and one in which we are not bigger than it, aggrandizing us unnecessarily.

In the panoramic view of the world surrounding us, we try to look at it and see it as its name implies, panoramically.

Looking at the vista in front of your eyes in this way, means that you gaze at nothing in particular, therefore, because your eyes do not focus on anything, everything that is there catches your attention in the same degree. There is no background and foreground and the attention to the view is broadened from the front of our eyes to the sides, almost to the corners of our eyes.

All of this brings an emphasized feeling of immediacy and freshness. It is as if everything is there for the first time and jumps into our attention with an innocent spontaneity. Since we do not concentrate on anything in particular, we are in a receptive mood. In this mood, we perceive everything unconditionally. We do not look at this or that, we just stare at all that is there, at all that the world has to offer to us at that moment. We do not choose anything to be the subject of an act of specific concentration; we do not treat anything in a preferential manner.

Moreover, suddenly we feel that besides seeing, the hearing takes a prominent role in the perception of the world, also. Like in a multi-media play, together with the sights, the sounds of our surroundings find their place in our awareness also, something of which we were not aware fully before, when we were looking at one object, focusing only on it. This is so because we do not concentrate our attention on anything in particular but look indiscriminatingly at everything in front of us.

Since there is nothing in the view before us trying to catch our attention as the only object in existence, everything there has its own equal presence; everything has an unquestionable right to be there. All things are equal in our eyes. Nothing is reduced to the background and on the other hand, nothing takes the front stage leaving all the others behind.

This is an important asset in the conscious effort not to compare and, therefore, not to be judgmental. More about this important subject will follow.

Another positive result of this tool is the immediate perception of a change and of a reduction in the notion that we entertain about the personal dimension that we occupy in this world, from a subjective one to an increase in the objective. This is true as to the physical self-perception, also.

When we stare passively, receptively, in front of us, as we do in the panoramic view, we change the roles of the participants in this interaction: From a role of an observer who gazes intently at the observed, we change to one who is contemplating the landscape that the Creation has to offer.

In this role, from an active entity that is projecting and directing its personal energy and attention out toward the world in a predetermined effort to grasp consciously only **one** of its myriad of components, we change into a passive receptacle, allowing itself to be inundated with everything that the world presents to us.

In the former role of a conscious observer looking at the observed, we are in a state of *duality* in which we are aware fully of *ourselves* versus the *other*, be it a person or an inanimate object. In the stage play onto which we projected ourselves, we occupy a disproportionate volume of our consciousness; we are at the center of it, together with the observed, and everything else is in the background. This is a subjective and distorted perception of us and of the other. In this perception, each one of the two entities engaged in such an interaction is prompted into foreground without real cause. Nothing in this Universe is more entitled than another thing to a more prominent place. By definition, everything in the Universe is equal to everything else. There is not such a thing as *better*, or *more important*. It is only our relative worldly perception of things that renders them as such.

In the new, passive and receptive role, we fall away from a center place in which we positioned ourselves unwarranted, as it is, and are relocated to a proper place, proportionate to the whole of the Universe. Likewise, the *other* is relocated correctly, also.

This simple and easy tool reduces both participants of this interaction, this stage play, to their proper dimensions and relocates them to their proper places in the Creation. Almost abruptly, we sense that our physical size is reduced to what seems all of a sudden to be its proper dimension. The world in our field of vision undergoes the same process, a reduction. And lo and behold, we feel good with it, as if something necessary was accomplished, something that puts all the pieces of the puzzle in their proper place.

Like with all the other tools in our toolbox, using this one produces also an altered state of mind, which in this case gives us a distinct feeling of a renewed connection with ourselves, a clean, calm and contented, righteous feeling of inner strength. It is as if we feel anchored in the most inner and deepest roots of ourselves. It is like coming home, something to which we aspire. In this process, we are performing like The Self, contemplating the world around us in an impersonal, non-judgmental way.

All this is sensed instantly and with strong authenticity, when practicing Panoramic View. The unconditional state in which we perceive the world around us can be sensed, literally. The perception is very real and it gives us a preview of what we can do in loving unconditionally, and, by association, in trying to forgive others and ourselves. We feel the immediacy and the freshness accompanying this perception of all that we see, we feel the reduction and the relocation of ourselves and of the other, of the world in front of us, and even beyond, to the proper size and place in the Universe. Finally, in addition to all this, there is the sharp feeling of coming back home, of reconnection with ourselves, with The Self in us.

This is, maybe, the most potent tool, besides meditation, in coming close to The Self, (re)connecting with it, really.

Now let us turn to the technique of viewing panoramically.

This can be done while sitting, or while walking or driving. As mentioned, the eyes stare in front of us at nothing in particular.

If we sit, then this is a little simpler. We just stare ahead, in front of us and, passively, switch from looking at one thing only, which means focusing on it, to allowing the world to fill us in its entirety, meaning that we stop focusing on that one thing only and disperse the attention to everything around.

Looking panoramically while walking or driving is a little different. As we look straight ahead into our field of view, our sight advances through the objects seen, from one to another, in the same pace as we walk or drive. That's all.

This type of viewing is not to be confused with meditation. Looking panoramically is not meditating, not in sitting and not in walking or driving. Meditation is a more complex process, which we shall meet in full in the following chapters.

Sex and Sexuality

In this passage, we shall reflect upon the role, negative and positive, that sex and sexuality have in the spiritual quest, if it is possible to employ it, and if yes, how to do it. Of concern to us in these terms, is their common meaning of interest in sexual activity and readiness for it, and participation in it. I shall not cover here the concept of sex as sinful, as perceived in some religions that shun it in principle but accept it for the purpose of procreation.

The matter of sex in spirituality is one of the most difficult subjects because of the antagonistic approaches to it and because of their implications to the question of how to live in the world of matter in which sex is one of the basic instinctual driving forces.

The stance gamut toward sex from the point of view of the spiritual quest covers the whole spectrum of possible attitudes and approaches. At one end, it runs from total abstinence in thought, word and deed, through full employment of sex but without seeking or achieving the ultimate pleasure that comes with it, the orgasmic climax. At the other end of the spectrum, sex is used with full anticipation of its accompanying and resulting pleasure, propounding that it is not an obstacle to the achievement of spirituality. Some in this extreme, dismiss entirely the notion of sex as spiritual obstacle, and believe that it is an efficient tool to be used toward this goal and do so.

It appears that from the earliest times humanity understood that in the context of the meanings mentioned at first—the interest in sexual activity, readiness for it and participation in it, sex and sexuality represent a most powerful and readily available energy, one that, paradoxically, was considered in two opposing ways, described above. In certain systems, it was suppressed, in others, employed actively. This last approach is represented in Tantrism, a Hindu and Buddhist spiritual approach, and in certain Western spiritual schools, known since the BC era as *The Mysteries*, described and, consequently, popularized in the last pages of the book *The Da Vinci Code*.

In most traditions, sex and sexuality are regarded until this very day as something that, if used, stands in the way of spiritual development as a most potent obstacle. In a few others, it is used actively to the advancement of spiritual development.

The former schools, those shunning active sex, propound total abstinence from it in whatever form sex may be exercised. The later, on the contrary, make use of it under various forms in quite elaborate ways, and teach methods to stimulate the sexual drive.

The reason for the attitudes of abstinence from sex goes to antiquity, thousands of years before our time. At its basis lies the belief that the mental and emotional, psychosomatic energy generated during the sexual act, can be used as a very potent catalyst in the spiritual endeavor. This energy is beneficial for the health and for the consciousness and is vital for the arduous task that the spiritual seeker takes upon himself when walking the path of the spiritual quest. Since those schools maintain that this energy is found mostly in the semen, they suggest total abstinence or at least a strict economical sexual activity, to contain it and the intrinsic energy in the body. This is true for both sexes, as it is believed that women produce a secretion similar to semen, also.

I would certainly suggest the adherence to a school that proposes abstinence or an economical sexual activity, as difficult and demanding as it may be, as a better way to fulfill the spiritual quest, while I disagree with the notion of free sex and with the use of sex approaches in spirituality, for two reasons.

One is the fact that through the lust that they stir in the rituals involved, one of the basic and most powerful instincts of the human being, the sex instinct, is excited, producing a desire that for a normal and healthy individual of both sexes is hard to overcome. Desire is the basic reason for the human suffering, therefore to be avoided as much as possible; there is no need to add to it beyond the natural state of the human existence by preconceived and periodical rituals.

The second reason is that the tapping of the natural human desire for sex by those schools, arouses unmistakably an expectation for the sexual process ritual that it involves, and excitement while participating in it, no matter how inadvertent and small they may be and how much they are controlled. Through those reenacted rituals, the repeated expectations and excitements develop attachment, which is something that we try to avoid. This attachment may reach a state of obsession for sex and addiction to it, certainly extremes to avoid. The distraction from the spiritual to the worldly that accompanies the sexual business in its totality, no matter how much it is held under control, is counterproductive to the ultimate goal.

Both schools can show great personal spiritual achievements, but, in the long term, the school that advocates abstinence will show that its approach is able to bestow a more advanced and permanent pursuit of the spiritual quest, one freer of obstacles than the other, much so.

So how do we abstain successfully when sex is such a forceful instinctual drive in the human life, our life, a drive that some find insurmountable, almost?

Fortunately, there are some tools, and because I do not believe in external devices, as you know by now, I shall not mention, for example, a plant called "Abraham's bush", which Christian monks in the Sinai desert, in Egypt, use to suppress their sexual appetite; I shall mention tools that are all in ourselves, in line with my self-sustenance stance.

The Talmud has a saying regarding sex:

"He who starves it, is sated; he who sates it, is hungry"

meaning that the more one has sex, the more he wants it, and the less he has it, the less he wants it. So very true. As always, those Rabbis know what they say.

As it turns out, a certain hormone in our body, produced in a certain natural and individual quantity level, regulates the sexual persistence. Now, the fact is that the more we give in to it, the more we produce it: The more we look around for a sexual object, ascertain and admire it, the more of this hormone is there to help us in our expectations, to be persistent in the sexual endeavor. The more we satisfy it, the more it is produced above the natural individual level. The more we suppress it, the less it is produced above this level. It reminds me of another saying: "He behaves like a pig! Give him a finger and he takes the whole hand!" This hormone is a piggy! The more you give to it, the more it grows in quantity and the more it wants. But unlike a pig, if you do not appease it, it will not yell, "I'm hungry, I'm hungry!" On the contrary, its natural individual measure will not be increased, so do not give to it, try to, ...well..., abstain, and, like everything else, little by little, you will train yourself not to give attention to anything to which you do not wish to grant. Nuns and monks vow to abstain; so do a number of Catholic laywomen worldwide, aptly named Consecrated Virgins, who, in an old Christian practice renewed in the late 20th century, wed themselves ceremonially to Christ and dedicate their lives to God, vowing to remain virgins for the rest of their lives. Their number is not great—in USA, today, late 2007, there are an estimated 200 consecrated women, while worldwide there are an estimated 3000 such women. But, as you can see, abstinence is adopted as a possible technique to enhance spirituality and practiced by quite a few.

Another tool is a certain section of the brain that controls concentration, focus and judgment, among other things. This section can function at various levels: high, moderate (or healthy), and low. Functioning on a low level, it produces a type of person who, from the point of view of compatibility in sex matters, is attracted indiscriminately toward sex and to the wrong objects of sexual attention. When coupled with high emotional activity, this cocktail is conducive to the development of sexual vices. Here, as in everything else in life, like with this piggy hormone above, training helps too, so train yourself to apply the right judgment, to stay focused, concentrated on the goal you had chosen—the quest for The Self.

Turn your eyes; avert them when they wander, when you feel that this particular pair of breasts, or this nice masculine, virile body, calls you from afar, from beyond the infinite distance between two total strangers. Lower the emotional level if it is too high. You will know when it is too high, for you can sense it. Apply the right judgment to what seems to attract you. Is it what you really want, what you really need? It is natural, it is human to fantasize and to dream, but is it right to pursue everything about which we fantasize or dream? Is it decent and in the frame of the accepted norms? Not everything is lawful, decent, or accepted. Try deliberately to abstain from sex or, if this is hard for you or if you have a companion in your life, use sex sparsely, in a strict economical manner and in its proper frame, one of mutual honor and respect, and keep it there, do not stray outside of it, looking for new excitements.

Little by little, training yourself in this way, the sex drive will be conquered. **It** will serve **you**, instead of you being the one who serves it, and you shall be able to channel its energy the way **you** want it, rightfully.

Quieting the loud voice of sexual passion in us, results in quieting us as a whole. It brings inevitably tranquility of body and mind. It is accompanied by a state of mind in which there is place for other things, too, besides the strong force of the sex drive, which absorbs so much of our attention.

Another helpful means to abstain is to do what is *needed*, instead of resisting what is *wanted*.

Resisting the drive to obtain or satisfy something we want is hard enough. Resisting an instinctual drive is much harder because it involves sheer suppression. Doing so with the powerful drive of sex is extremely hard. Maybe it would be a good idea if we tried to bypass it, somehow, instead of suppressing it. Let us see how.

Instead of trying to ignore its call and to achieve abstinence by resisting and suppressing it, do what is needed: Approach abstinence from the point of view of short- and long-term goals. Look at it from the point of view of the necessity for conserving this energy because you need it, which is a long-term goal, not from the point of view that abstaining from sex now will not spend the needed energy, which is a short-term goal. Trying to avoid something that is already there is harder than trying to attain a remote goal.

This is exactly what we do when we try not to spend now

versus trying to save for the future, bypassing the spending desire for a future advantageous goal. This switch of thinking is not just intellectual gymnastics; it provides a helpful psychological perspective for any kind of abstinence.

Another similar example would be the situation in which I am hungry and I want to eat, but in half an hour the Thanksgiving dinner will be ready. By applying this thinking switch, instead of resisting the hunger while it pinches me, sticking my belly to my back, making every second an eternity of hell until dinner is served, I am going to say to myself that in just a little while food is available, therefore it would be a bit foolish to eat at this very moment. By the time the dinner is served, I shall be full and unable to enjoy the food and the company in the way the host and I intended to enjoy; I may even eat in spite of being full, already, which will be unpleasant. By this switch of thought, I take into consideration my short-and long-term goals. I shall not try to resist the immediate pressure of the instinctive drive of hunger, which is hard to suppress, especially when all I have to do is to grab some snacks and swallow them whole. I shall make it easier for myself not to eat by bypassing the desire and looking at it from the point of view of what I need to do at this time, the perspective of the long-term goal.

Sex abstinence is possible, at least in some measure, but if it is hard to achieve, there is still the alternative of economic sex, therefore, it should not be an insurmountable obstacle; there is nothing, really, that our will cannot achieve.

Signs of Finding and Reuniting with The Self

After perusing the various tools available, you might want to ask how would you know that you had reached The Self. Frankly, I do not have a definitive answer to this question and I do not believe there is someone who knows it.

However, besides some circumstantial evidence upon which I touched here and there previously, and shall do so again more detailed, shortly, a certain source points to some physical evidence to this effect.

In one of the Upanishads—early Hindu spiritual scriptures preceding the religious ones, the Svetasvatara, it is mentioned that if one sees lights of various kinds while meditating (understood, of course, as doing it with closed eyes), then he is on his way to The Self.

Well, I thought well and long about this postulate because, at the time, it intrigued me very much, and it still does, especially in the light of the answer I propose, which may be wrong, of course.

However, if, by any chance, my answer holds water, then the question of what is the materialistic basis for our *consciousness*, a question represented in the conventional science by the *Neurobiology of Conscience*, a nascent academic discipline, may be a bit clearer. I had not read, yet, any paper in this field, so I do not know if my answer is supported scientifically. If it is, then I am in good company and this question has an answer, finally. Again, what follows is only my intuitive personal assumption, coming from a nonprofessional person, with no claim whatsoever that it is accurate. My explanation is as follows.

In all the spiritual sources that deal with this issue, The Self is described always as self-luminous, as the light within the fire, the light of the eternal consciousness, as opposed to the consciousness of the cognitive, daily intelligence, that of the worldly ego. Therein lies my non-professional, hypothetical explanation.

When the senses are disconnected, as in the stage of deep meditative concentration (to be dealt with later in the chapter about Meditation), the nervous system maintains only its purely basic activity, and it is only this activity that "holds" the body, as if it is holding its molecules together to enable the body to function. This effect is called *sensory deprivation*.

The measure of this sensory reduction is in direct proportion to the measure of the concentration and of the resulting sensory deprivation that the seeker achieves while meditating.

Being almost totally disconnected, the senses do not send stimuli, or send only a few if only a smaller disconnection has been achieved. This results in a reduction, or even a cancellation, of certain types of control that the nervous system is having on the body. This is not a total cancellation, as if the body was paralyzed, but a barrier that the sensory deprivation puts between the body and the surrounding world, enabling the meditator, as a result, to be oblivious to the auditory and tactile stimuli, mainly.

In this reduced and specific control of the nervous system, the meditator is able to perceive the electrical connections that are constantly present between the brain neurons. He perceives them in one of their physical aspects, *light*. Such lights are called *phosphenes* and are caused by random firing of the cells in the visual system, as also when rubbing the eyes. He is able to do so, presumably, because now, upon the absence of the external sensory stimuli, some inner perception channels of physical phenomena, which were not available until this moment of disconnection of the senses, or were overridden by cognizing the external world, are freed and come to the fore being fired involuntarily by the organism, and sensed. We shall come again, in due course, to the theme of 'lights' seen when concentrated.

In this specific case of sensory deprivation, the substance of this physical phenomena perception, the lights seen, constitute a reflective influence of our higher consciousness, because, if the senses are disconnected and overridden, what else can be there to activate the nerves and their synapses, the neurons and their axons, and so, to be perceived?

If the lower, cognitive consciousness that is responsive to the **external** stimuli is disconnected partially or totally, then, all that is at our disposal and which we are able to perceive are some physical phenomena that are the result of some other, **inner**, physical activity. This inner physical activity should include not only the nervous system control of the basic bodily activity, but also the control that this system exerts over the mental process, for it cannot be that this system does not have a mental aspect of influence.

If this is so, then it may very well constitute the explanation for the lights one "sees" when in deep concentration, or prolonged quietude, and which the Svetasvatara Upanishad defines as signs on the way to The Self and of reaching it.

This may well be also the explanation for the **sounds** that are heard in such altered states of mind. Such sounds can be a noisy hum, loud, and sometimes explosive.

So, when in a state of deep concentration, which results in a state of sensory deprivation, there appear perceptible inner lights and sounds.

To hear the sounds and to see the extremely luminous inner lights of all shapes and sizes, try a certain yogic exercise, the *mudra* (a yogi technique) of "*shan-mukhi* (six-openings)". In this exercise, the ears, the eyes and the nostrils are blocked, so the senses involved are deprived. Use both hands. With closed mouth, put your thumbs in the ears, put your index fingers on the closed eyes, and, finally, put your third fingers on the nostrils, keeping them all tightly shut. Tell me what you hear and see!

Another physical sign of reaching a higher level of consciousness through intensified concentration and sensory deprivation is the involuntary tremor and rocking of the body, which can be quite violent, and, ultimately, involuntary levitation, the act of rising and floating in the air, defying gravity. Levitation, otherwise, can be intentional, and, like other super-natural abilities, is achieved as an almost automatic result of a high stage of spiritual development, which in turn affects the bodily development.

Rocking of the body, or shaking, or tremors, occur quite often when in such a state of mind. They may appear in the form of a slight swaying of the body, or be quite violent. It starts from the head and spreads to the whole body. If sitting when it happens, it affects the upper body.

Levitation is reached through the same process and is an extreme form of the reduced control of the nervous system on the physical body. The Eastern spiritual scriptures and the advertisements of the modern Transcendental Meditation movement, claim that this fit is possible and that it happens.

These phenomena are possible because of the same reason explained above for the light visions and the apparent sounds.

There are other signs, as I mentioned in the beginning of this section. Those signs are of a developmental and personal disposition nature.

A deep and intense sense of freedom, improved performance in every field of life, bliss, ability to empathize, to be humble and feel compassion, are such signs and can be safely counted as the most important of them.

Some of them, like empathy, humbleness, compassion and the like, are personal qualities, which can develop and may be present in any individual striving to be a better human being, just a good person above the average. The spiritual process, however, whether it is a conventional religious practice anchored in the established religions teachings, or the quest for The Self, which may not be religiously related, sharpens such qualities and brings them to the fore in an intensified and concentrated form. It makes the particular person acutely aware of these qualities and of the imperative necessity to make them a permanent part of the personal awareness and consciousness, and to apply them in the daily life. The presence of an acute awareness of these signs is the real indication of the advancement in this quest. The driving motive behind this acuteness is the pronounced feeling of unity with everyone and everything, which is at the basis of this quest.

The first three signs, a very real and sharp sense of freedom, a sense of bliss and an improved performance in every field of life, are new personal achievements resulting from the spiritual process involved in this quest, and genuine. Usually, they are not present before this process is undertaken, when they may appear in the human consciousness only casually, accidentally. Those casual instances are transformed by the spiritual process into recurring experiences, on a more or less permanent basis, reappearing almost at will, mainly during the meditative process, or in spiritual actions that involve physical exercises, such as various kinds of Yoga.

The sense of freedom comes to the seeker in the wake of the liberation of the senses from the yoke of this world of matter for brief or more prolonged moments, if only temporarily.

The feeling of bliss is a predetermined consequence of such freedom. It has an unmistakable nature, which one cannot err in recognizing, and which does not need any external proof for its presence. It is there, and the seeker knows beyond doubt that it is there. Putting it simply, in this state, the seeker is filled to the brim with a silent and confident feeling of an immeasurable happiness. An inner smile, profound and embracing all, confronting the world peacefully and from a point of vantage, inundates him. This feeling comes to him **automatically** because of the freedom attained.

The improved performance stems from the fact that the seeker is much more concentrated and self-observant in what he is doing; therefore, he is planning and executing his actions in a better fashion.

Other signs will be evident as well.

The seeker will experience an increased and pronounced personal magnetism, which will serve as a source of attraction in personal relationships and as a font of energy for all around, who will be unable to define what is it that they feel but feel they do.

His eloquence and ability to understand new and complicated things will be enhanced in a surprising measure, to the point of wonder, almost.

These signs are proof that something is changing in us, and though no one can say with certainty that they are proof for attaining The Self and reuniting with it, those symptoms of change serve as circumstantial evidence that we are indeed on the right way. We are engaged in the spiritual quest and use certain tools on our way, so the changes observed should be a result of this conscious use of such tools.

All these signs are direct results of the spiritual undertaking and are unmistakably clear and obvious to the person experiencing them and to others who observe him or interact with him.

Having covered the technicalities of the spiritual quest, we turn, now, to the subject of meditation, and first, to the question of why is meditation such a valuable tool in the spiritual quest, valuable to the point of indispensability.

Chapter Three

The First W of M - Why Meditation

...

The best Tool in our Quest for the Divine within

Walking The Way to our Self is a declaration of sorts on our part. It tells others, the world, and ourselves that we are on a quest, and a very special one for that matter, a quest in which we want to contact The Self and to reunite with it. In this quest, to enhance its efficiency, we employ various tools, like the ones described in the previous chapter, and more, as the seeker sees fit.

All these tools have a decided influence on us. This influence is what makes the "walking" declaratory, because it shows outwardly and others feel it, even if in an undefined way.

One of these tools is Meditation. I maintain that this tool is the best of them; if I were to choose only one of the important practical tools mentioned in Ch. Two, I would choose this one. Why, what makes it the best?

The first, direct and immediate reason is that we are the temple in which the individual Self, our own part of the Universal Self, resides, thus, we are in a position in which we can contact it directly, immediately and without an intermediary. In this, meditation serves as the direct tool. The second reason is that meditation is of tremendous help in the pursuit of self-knowledge, and thus, knowledge of the world.

"Know yourself, and you shall know the whole world"

Everything that keeps us on the track of reunion with The Self and reminds us constantly of this legacy is suitable for our use. For the purpose of direct communication with The Self, we can quite easily employ religion. We can do so in its most conventional forms—worship, prayer and devotion, calling upon God as another expression of Self, and petitioning Him, adoring Him all the while, praising Him. However, for the purpose of the reunification with The Self, the religious means of reaching it has a dual nature that by definition puts a distance between it and us.

The situation in which we consciously stand before God, The Supreme Self, the object and place we call home, and turn our eyes to it and pray to, or adore from afar, from the fields of this world, turns us both, God and us, into two entirely separate entities. Without recognizing the basic noble human responsibility to reunite with The Self and making the effort to implement it, this form of connection is unsuitable, therefore, to the reunification quest upon which we engage. Remember, be with Him and watch this world, instead of being here and yearning for Him.

To achieve both aims, that is, connecting directly to The Self and reuniting with it upon reaching it, another tool is necessary, even if only temporarily, one that in some way can achieve these two goals at the same time. Meditation is such kind of tool. Actually, I do not know of any other means that can fulfill satisfactorily these ample and profound tasks by being used solely. So much so that Buddha said that we have to aim to be in a state of constant meditation.

Meditation has a central, fundamental role in this kind of quest, used either as the only tool or in combination with others, lesser ones, and is recognized as such. For example, in the East, mainly in India, there are many houses, which, even in the smallest of them, have a small space reserved for it. In Tibet, at least before the Communist regime, there were special houses dedicated to passers-by who wished to meditate.

It must be stated right away that meditation can be used in a religious context, or separately, unconnected at all to religion. This versatility makes it a suitable tool for anyone who walks the spiritual way, in whatever form, according to the personal inclination.

Though the subject of meditation itself will be covered later in detail in specific chapters, of interest to us, now, as additional answers to the question "Why Meditation", are the particular qualities that make it such a powerful and efficient tool in the quest for The Self. These qualities are *convenience, concentration, sensory deprivation* and *facilitation of self-knowledge and of the world.*

Its *convenience* is obvious, as it needs absolutely nothing else besides time and a little place. There are a few basic rules to follow, if a certain measure of efficiency is desired, but, ultimately, a few minutes and a little corner are all one needs. *Concentration* is part of the meditative process. *Sensory deprivation* is a direct result of this specific part. Both shall be explained later, but a few general words about them are in order, now.

Concentration is a state of mind in which we are engaged in a careful and specifically directed attention. It can be achieved quite easily, relatively, and in the most trivial of situations. If done in earnest, the smallest and most insignificant task can be conducive to the deepest concentration. Such a sharp and concentrated focus brings an immediate and direct result. It diverts the attention away from the general and permanent scope of the involuntary cognitive perception of the surrounding world, with its hypnotic influence, to the temporary point of focus of our concentrative powers, whatever this project may be.

In this state of concentration, the meditator is ready to focus on the goals of the meditation process that, ultimately, after discarding the world around him, are nothingness and oneness with The Self.

Sense deprivation is a by-product of the deep concentration in which the meditator is engaged. Focusing so intensely on the meditation goals, he is oblivious, almost, to the outer world and its stimuli. The sole point of anchor of his whole being is somewhere near him, in his field of consciousness, of awareness. This point is located about half a foot away from his third eye, in the void perceptible to him when he meditates with open or closed eyes. This will be clearer later on, in the chapter describing how to meditate.

The attainment of the goals mentioned in the beginning, that is, the direct communication with The Self and reuniting with it, can be, by definition, only temporary, as was stated implicitly and directly a few times already. This, of course, is because of the basic reason that as long as we live in the physical body, we dwell in this world as an inseparable part of it. We cannot expect to reunite with The Self permanently, while being in our physical body. Bearing in mind this basic understanding of our quest and its results, meditation is the best tool: It is the simplest and the most efficient. It enables us to experience the highest number of instances of being with The Self and of the longest duration.

As mentioned, and worth repeating, meditation is also of great importance and help in advancing our knowledge of ourselves and of the world, because of the reflective process in which we are engaged while doing it. This is a very important aspect of meditation and of the quest for The Self.

Besides these extremely positive and important qualities, meditation, like spirituality, is decisively adding to the personal development of the meditator in many positive ways, which will be detailed in the last chapter. There is no domain of the personal make-up left unaffected by the influence of meditation. It is an extremely valuable tool; it is readily available for use, it is of an infinite supply and it brings almost immediate results in so many domains.

From here, we go to our next goal, which is to explain in detail the mechanism of meditation.

Chapter Four

The Second W of M – What is Meditation

. . .

The Mechanism of Meditation

In answering the invariable question of "How do I meditate", I, invariably also, start with the explanation of what is meditation, because a correct understanding of its mechanism is of great importance in performing it. This is what I shall do here.

To begin with, meditation is a reflective state of mind in which we enjoy a great measure of freedom from the outside world, and though while performing it we may reflect on this very world among other subjects, we try deliberately to cut any tie with it, at least during the meditation session.

Subsequently, the *meditative process*—for it is a process, and a structured one for that matter, a statement that will be explained shortly—enables us to know ourselves and the world and to enjoy a strongly perceived state of inner peace and boundless unity that permeates our entire being. This state of mind, I hasten to clarify, should never be confused with a state of trance.

This psychic condition is a direct result of reducing the frame of the conscious perception of ourselves to a small area in our being. This area is the field of our perception during meditation; it is well defined and quite restricted.

Focusing on this point while meditating, the world ceases to exist for us in a measure commensurate with the intensity and depth of our concentration. This condition of highly focused concentration is perceived as what can be defined concisely as "*Bliss in Unity*". If this is the case, why "Meditation" then, why not "Reflection"; or, for that matter, "Blissful Meditation", or "Blissful Reflection (as in 'thinking')", or even "Blissful Relaxation", if this state of being is characterized as reflective, thoughtful, pure and deep, blissful, characterized by inner peace and unity?

The answer to this question is that *meditation* (or *reflection*), and *relaxation*, are two distinct, sequential stages of a practice that includes them as partial activities and also as immediately following partial results; the overall and final result of it all, being the above-mentioned *unity* accompanied by a *blissful inner peace*. This effect, the ensuing sense of unity, is the ultimate goal of the meditative process, when used as a tool in our quest for The Self.

Although, obviously, someone started it at some point, it is not known who this person was or where was it initiated – though it would be interesting to know who did it first, when and where, but it is safe to say that the practice of meditation is thousands of years old. It would also be fair to assume that, as it happens with so many starters, it occurred to more than one person and in more than one place in different times or in the same time, when those persons engaged in a spiritual activity, and more especially so, in prayer.

This is a process that, in principle, anyone can approach freely, in any way he likes, without any restriction whatsoever of any form, sequence, time, place, or mood; it would be better, though, to do it systematically. A seasoned meditator can go directly to one of the last three *stages*—to be explained immediately—at will, and be *relaxed* and *concentrated* almost instantly; the beginner is advised to undertake consciously the first two stages before attempting to *meditate* and, more so, to *contemplate* and, eventually, to engage in the final, optional stage of *adoration*.

Despite the fact that meditation is what appears to be a natural activity, this is a conscious and voluntary process that can be defined accurately.

It is a *Hierarchically Structured Process*, defined, for the first time, by the author.

When performed fully, it includes five sequential *Stages*, one of which, the last, is optional: *Relaxation, Concentration, Meditation, Contemplation* and *Adoration*. The first two stages are preparatory, in advance of the last three, of which Contemplation is the culmination.

During the *Relaxation* stage, the meditator is doing just that—he relaxes. The purpose of this stage is to prepare himself for the stage of *Concentration.*

In the *Concentration* stage, the meditator concentrates his mental faculties and his physical focus for the *Meditation, Contemplation,* and the optional *Adoration,* stages.

While in the *Meditation* stage, the meditator reflects on a subject of his choosing, abstract or concrete, trying to achieve knowledge of self and of the world. This is a very important result of the meditation process.

In the *Contemplation* stage, the meditator is engaged in just contemplating the subject on which he reflected a moment ago in the Meditation stage, or another subject of his choosing, abstract or concrete. Alternatively, he can just stare in the void of nothingness in the field of vision while his eyes are closed (as advised in general in meditation, regarding posture and bodily position).

This is the most important stage in the process. In this stage, we reach the closest proximity to the goal of the quest—finding the Self and being one with it, and we may even achieve it in some rare moments of a rather short duration, usually, as mentioned before in a few instances. But, to reiterate, just as an aside much needed clarification, as long as we are in this world, a permanent reunification with The Self is impossible.

In the final and optional Adoration stage, the meditator engages himself in adoring God, or, less preferable but perfectly legitimate, a person of high spiritual standing. This stage is optional because adoring God concerns believers, while directing the attention of non-believers to an individual of high spiritual standing would put the action more in the contemplation aspect, for non-attachment reasons.

Like in many other named processes or staged, sequential activities, the meditative process takes its name after its most conspicuous stage, Meditation.

When approached systematically, this process has two parts. The first part of the meditation process includes the Relaxation and the Concentration stages. It is a preamble for the much more intense stages of Meditation, Contemplation and (the optional stage of) Adoration, the stages of its second part. There is logic behind this, the basis for which is the answer to the question of what are the best means to employ in order to meditate successfully.

To understand this, we only have to look at the meaning of the name of its namesake stage, the Meditation stage, and at the question of what we need to do in order to meditate successfully. The reason and the need for such a sequence will appear, then, as a natural outcome.

The meaning of the word *meditation* is "to think or to reflect, calmly and deliberately".

As with any other action, to do it successfully, certain conditions are necessary. If we consider something, reflecting on it, if we want to think clearly with good results, it would be good to be in a certain state of mind and body. Now, just a moment! Body? Mind is understandable, but body too? Yes, body too! How many times we said, "I can't think. It's so noisy here. The chair is so uncomfortable". To understand why it is necessary to prepare ourselves for a successful and fruitful meditative state of mind, let us take the process backward, from the meditative stage to the beginning of the process. Once there, all will be clear.

So let us go backward. To think about a solution for a problem, to consider something successfully, or, in short, to meditate, we have to be concentrated, but to be concentrated we need to be relaxed—stress is counterproductive to concentration. To be relaxed, though, we need to be undistracted as best as possible, and there we are, at the beginning of the meditative process, understanding the necessity of the first two, sequential stages.

From this initial point, we go now forward, to the Meditation stage. Trying to eliminate possible distractions, we aim to relax, physically and mentally, and so, we enable ourselves to concentrate as deeply as possible; then, being concentrated, we can meditate successfully.

Obviously, then, an *absence of distractions* (as complete as possible), a state of *relaxation* (as deep as possible), and then, a state of *concentration* (again, as deep as possible), are **The** prerequisites here and we have to follow them in this seemingly natural order.

There are a myriad of stimuli out there, determined to lead us astray by distracting us. If our body is irritated by a mosquito or by an uncomfortable seat, if thirst or hunger nag us, then it will be rather hard to think. Likewise, things of the mind: If thoughts about every possible thing that affects our life torment us—family, work, bills, affairs of the heart, then it is hard, if not impossible, to think coherently about something. We must, then, get rid of the distraction first, or, if this is impossible, try not to pay attention to it. One cannot just jump into meditation, at least not in the beginning. As already mentioned, a seasoned meditator can do so, but only because he had done it many times before, so his mental faculties and bodily functions are preconditioned to it; he can begin the meditative stage almost at will, skipping the first two stages of relaxation and concentration. A beginner should approach the meditation systematically.

The question of how do we know that we are concentrated enough to start meditating is decided on the spot. After many sessions of meditation, the experience starts to show and we are able to decide instinctively that we are concentrated enough to begin meditating. Likewise, the time when the meditation stage ends and the contemplation stage begins, is a matter of personal feeling.

If, just for the sake of curiosity, one keeps the time, there will come a day when he will see that each stage starts at the same time, ends after the same length of time, and the whole session ends after the same length of time: The meditator became conditioned. This is the time when he can start meditating or contemplating without any preparations—he is able to bring himself instantly into the relaxed state of mind and body that, in its turn, enables almost instant concentration.

The meditation session ends with the Contemplation stage and an optional continuation is the Adoration stage.

Having covered the subject of "What is Meditation", the natural course of attention will take us to the inevitable question of how to do it. The next chapter reviews it extensively. It is my hope and belief that after reading it, you will be left with no questions about it. I invite you, then, to the meditation room.

Chapter Five

The Other Two Ws of M – When and Where

...

The Environment of Meditation and Other Related Matters

Knowing the mechanism of meditation, its role in spirituality and the link between the two, in order to enable a successful and pleasant meditating experience we now turn our attention to its practical aspects, which constitute its environmental envelope.

In this regard, a few basic demands are in order. They can be defined as the physical and mental environmental conditions that one strives to establish before meditating. These demands are to be met in a more or less organized and disciplined manner, so the meditation session will be performed as much as possible in an unobstructed way. The intention here is not to impose a rigid disciplinarian set of rules but, again, to make it pleasant and efficient. These rules present the *ideal* conditions in which we would like to meditate.

Those requests are the *Time of Day*, the *Physical Ambience*—place and seat, temperature, permanence and sanctity, the *Clothing*, the *Body Posture and Facial Demeanor*—head and hands holding and face pose, the *Mental Attitude*, and, finally, the *Breathing*. These various factors of the environment of meditation are chosen carefully so they will be the most comfortable and the most suitable to use. That said, it should be remembered that this is a free activity in all its aspects, and for the one who cannot find or establish the suitable conditions, or does not care about it, any different performance is perfectly acceptable. Although all are important factors, any time or place, any kind of clothes, posture and breathing, are welcome and acceptable without any reservation. Ultimately, the only thing of real importance here is the right mental attitude.

Time

The best *time* for meditation is the very early hours of the day, before dawn. Midnight can be a good alternative. Any other time will do also, but it should be the choice of last resort.

These early hours, defined as the best, have a particular tranquil and reclusive quality that is felt instinctively and which is conducive to the meditative state of mind more than others. They are not hectic as the rest of the day is in some measure or other; by avoiding those "rush hours", we escape the likelihood of being caught in their fever.

Physical Ambience

The *place* that we choose to use for our meditation sessions should be dedicated solely for the purpose of meditation; preferably, no other task should be performed there, even if it is only a small corner in a room. If this can be achieved, then a sense of *permanence* will be attached to it; this will enhance the meditating experience. In such a place, the meditator is able to find shelter from the surrounding world—the more secluded, the better.

Obviously, this place should be private, quiet and comfortable; I would define it as cozy, almost.

To impart to it an atmosphere of *sanctity* before it is used for the first time, it should be consecrated and purified of strange and negative energy. This can be done by an invocation, a sentence or a phrase to this effect, or a song.

You may do this by standing in front of this place, with your palms open and directed toward it; then, with reverence and pure intention, aloud or in the quiet of your heart, whatever you may think is appropriate, say for example, "I dedicate this place for my meditation sessions; may I enjoy peace of mind and may my heart be pure while I meditate therein". To this personal and abstract kind of consecration, we may add external and concrete additions—candles, incense, a pinch of salt in the corners of the room, chimes, little bells, consecrated small pieces of stone or wood, or anything else that suits us. For a positive and benevolent inspiration, you may add a picture or a statuette of your personal guru, of a revered saint or another guru. You can also contemplate on this picture or statuette – in line with the freedom you may exercise in the meditation process, this can be considered a meditation session in itself, consisting of the contemplation part, only. As a reminder for those interested or touched by this issue, it is forbidden in Judaism and in stricter forms of Islam, to make and to revere pictures or statues, which is considered idolatry.

In time, our continued daily presence in this place in a meditative state of mind and practicing it, the elated positive energies and vibrations emanating from us will add to the place and imbue it with them. Together with the consecration we imparted to it, the place used for meditation will be pure and sanctified, supporting us in the meditation process and emanating further, to its surroundings.

The *seat*, applicable in sitting meditating postures, should be flat, horizontal and soft, because after a while, and certainly after a long meditating session, the coccyx bone starts to ache from so much sitting. The seat can be a chair, a bench, or just the edge of a bed.

The *temperature* in this room should be pleasant and comfortable, not too warm and not too cold.

Clothing

The clothes worn while meditating should be comfortable, not rough nor pressing; if we meditate in the open and the situation calls for it, they should insulate from cold or heat and from bugs.

If the personal preference is to meditate naked or in our underwear, then, by all means, in our own privacy we are free to do it without any reservations and inhibitions.

Physical Posture

Regarding the physical posture, the meditation can be done in any manner we desire or during any physical activity—sitting, lying, walking, running, swimming, flying, making love, you name it. Here, we shall deal with the basic positions, the *stationary* ones: the *lotus* sitting—*full* and *half*, the *cross-legged* and the *plain* sitting, and the *lying down* postures. All of the others mentioned before, are creative expansions of meditation into the dominion of movement in all its forms, except in Tantrism where it is employed during mundane acts as a specific tool.

For reasons that will be explained shortly, the preferred and original meditating postures are the full- and half-lotus and the cross-legged positions, though experienced meditators maintain that this is hard for Westerners to do, especially for a prolonged time, the lotus position in particular. If you can, then it is very good, but if these positions are undesired, we can choose from the sitting or the lying positions.

The full-, the half-lotus and the cross-legged positions are most suited for meditating for two reasons. First, in these positions, our extremities are in the closest possible range to each other and to the rest of our body, including the head. In these positions, our body is a bundle centered on our solar plexus. This way, we maintain a rounded, closely-knit energy reactor, in which the energy flows freer between its various ends. Second, in this manner we maintain an almost perfect balance, which is important for an obvious reason: Seated on a firm foundation, we are not prone to fall forward or backward. How is this done?

In the full-lotus position, the outer side of one foot is put upon the inner side of the other knee, or thigh; in the half-lotus position, the right or left foot is put **on** the other knee or thigh and the other foot **under** the opposite knee or thigh; this compromise makes it easier to sit in the lotus position.

The cross-legged pose, a natural posture, is easier, so it can be used as a substitute for the lotus poses. In this posture, you just cross your legs one under the other, while sitting.

For all these three positions, sitting on the floor or on a bed is best, obviously; a chair would be too narrow.

Be notified, though, that, in these positions, the knees are contorted, so they are under much tension for quite a prolonged period, which is unhealthy. After many sessions of meditation in this fashion, the knees are in danger of being damaged.

While each style has its own merits, health and personal inclination are to be taken into consideration also, as anything that goes contrary to our well-being is to be reconsidered and maybe discarded. This general rule of thumb is dismissed when one practices asceticism. Then, when performing harsh practices of mind and body, it is acknowledged that there will be an initial or even continuous period in which there will be unpleasant or even harsh physical or mental experiences, or both of them, until the particular exercise is assimilated into one's physical and mental constitution.

From the other two postures left for Western meditators to employ, the sitting and the lying down, let us deal with this of lying down, first.

This position is exactly what it says, meditating while lying down. Because meditating in general can lull us easily due to the inner tranquility and the prolonged silence, doing it while lying down is not recommended much in this regard. There is always a possibility of falling asleep during meditation in any position; obviously, the possibility of falling asleep while lying down is greater than in any other position, so it should be avoided. This aspect is very real, so much so that, in some Zen and Buddhist monasteries, there are 'police monks' who are assigned with the specific task of awakening the ones who fall asleep. They do this by a blow on the back of the sleepy meditator with a club that the constantly patrolling disciplining monk holds in his hand. And they are meditating while sitting, mind you, so imagine how many beaten spiritual bodies would be if they did it while lying down.

Anyway, let us see how it is done and you will decide if you want to do it that way. In the lying position, the person lies with his hands alongside or on the chest, below the neck and over the heart, the left palm resting over the right one and the thumbs adjoined at their tips to ensure a continuous energetic circle.

Now, if the lotus and cross-legged postures can damage our knees and lying down may make us sleep, then let us meditate in the best fitting position of the three stationary ones, the sitting posture, which does not cause contortion of the knees and in which we are less prone to fall asleep.

We shall try to do it in a way that will maintain the best and most stable balance and the best energy flow possible.

While *sitting*, the body forms a set of straight lines with right angles: erect back, straight thighs, forming an L, and legs bent at the knees, with feet flat on the floor, forming another L, the whole body taking a final shape of └L. The 'straight lines and right angles' posture helps to keep good balance and straight energy lines.

The sitting itself should be done in a way that enlarges to the greatest extent the area of the body on which we sit, providing the largest and most stable spot.

When we sit, we do so by putting the body weight on three points, forming what looks as a triangle: the two buttocks, and the coccyx bone. This area can be expanded by enlarging it. This is accomplished in the following way. Shifting the weight of the body on the right buttock, we move the left one as far as possible to the side; shifting, now, the weight of the body on the left buttock, we move the right one as far as possible to the side. Now, sitting on the two more distanced buttocks, we move backwards a bit and place ourselves on the coccyx bone. Doing so, we sit, now, on three firmly placed spots, forming a triangle, as mentioned. This kind of sitting gives a larger and more stable area, thus giving to the lower back and to the whole body a better support.

The *head* is held erect, also, keeping in line with the erect upper body, and bent slightly forward, until it forms a straight line with the nape. This position is very comfortable; the head is not leaning backwards sluggishly, a posture that exerts pressure on the neck and the spine; it bestows a dignified erect posture to the upper body, adding what may be defined as a respectable attitude. We can actually feel the difference in attitude if, after tilting our head slightly backwards in a relaxed way or just hold it there, relaxed and careless, we tilt it forward as explained.

The *hands* rest on the thighs, with palms on the knee and open upwards. The thumbs touch the index finger, forming an "o", another attempt to keep a close energy flow circuit. Another position of the palms would be to put them in our lap, open upwards, the right one over the left one, forming an open bowl, with thumbs touching each other to form a close energy circuit.

The *facial* pose deals with the eyes and the mouth, including the tongue and the lips.

This pose varies and can be wide-open, half-open, and closed eyes and mouth.

There are those who meditate with the eyes and the mouth open, or with open eyes and closed mouth or vice versa. Some will meditate with the lips barely touching each other, or with the tongue touching the palate to prevent excessive salivation when the mouth is open.

Each person should choose the style that fits him the best. For example, if one has problems breathing only through the nose, then an open mouth is to be preferred, of course.

While on the subject of facial pose, it is timely to touch on a certain aspect of it, one that appears during meditation, especially in a prolonged session and when the concentration is deeper.

After a while, the lower lip pushes against the upper and the mouth contracts a little. This is accompanied, sometimes, with a contraction of the eyes and a tilt of the head backwards.

Some think that this is a sign of something of a higher spiritual note, but this is not so. I have no proof for the explanation that I am about to present for this phenomenon, as I am not an expert in these matters, but, to the best of my knowledge, the contraction of the lips together influences the brain. This is known from observing babies who are breast-fed—and, by the way, this is why it is so important to feed a baby from its mother's breast: The contraction of the lips and the whole mouth is much more pronounced than in bottle-feeding; this enhances the baby's mental development. From this, it appears that the phenomenon mentioned is a reverse reaction to the high state of concentration of the meditating person: Through a feedback process, the concentration, in its turn, triggers the physical activity that promotes it.

The tilt of the head backwards is caused by the fact that the meditator is instinctively focusing most of the time on a point that is located where the 'third eye' is thought to be, between the eyes and just above the nose, inside the head. By the mere continuous attention to that point, the head follows the direction in which this attention is pointing, which is upward. After a while, the head tilts upward, too, and then, backward, because it is not possible to move the head upward anymore.

Another little phenomenon that is worth our consideration is the inward direction that the focus of our attention takes after a while. Little by little, from the point of the third eye, the focus turns inward, inside our skull, and after a while, it appears that we look at our own eyes; then, a sense of pressure is felt in them because of the shortening of the eyes' focus. Some instruct specifically not to look inward, but, from my experience, I see no real reason why. We should strive to focus our attention to the 'third eye' point, it being the point of connection between the higher spiritual world and us, a subject to be touched later, but any other point is fine, if we feel good with it.

Mental Attitude

The attitude to be assumed throughout the meditative process is one in which we are neither over-expectant nor apathetic, but retain ourselves in a quiet state of alertness. This should be remembered always. It is the attitude of the wise. He is always on quiet alert, listening and seeing, and then, reacting, but only when needed, unnoticed, if possible.

Breathing

We reach, now, the last point to be covered in the chapter that deals with the environment of meditation. This section deals with the important subject of *breathing*.

Even though, ultimately, during meditation one can breathe without controlling the breath, doing it freely, as professed with everything performed in the spiritual quest, none of the various aspects of meditation perused above is as important as breathing.

The immediate reason for its significant importance is that there is a mutual influence between it and the flow of thoughts, the great foe of inner peace. The pace of each one is a direct outcome of that of the other.

Yet another reason for the breathing importance is the (human) ability to influence the body and to induce and control diverse states of mind by controlling it, an ability noticed since ancient times.

Adding to the arguments for using the breath as an efficient means for inner peace and for control of the mind and of the body, is the fact that it is equated with *soul* and, by implication, with *self.*

The etymology of the word *breath* will tell us quite much in this regard. In Indo-European languages, the word breath – for example, *spirare,* in Latin – lent its root to the word *spirit,* which, essentially, means *soul* or *self.* In Sanskrit, another Indo-European language, the word *prana* means *breath, soul* and *self,* among other related meanings. Likewise, in Hebrew, a Semitic language, the words for *breathing*—"neshimah" and *soul*—"neshamah", share the same root, "n-sh-m"; the word "ruakh" ('kh' as guttural 'h') in Hebrew is *wind,* but it is also used for *spirit.*

Thus, since breath is clearly associated with The Self, and since The Self is incorruptible and, therefore, incapable of doing evil and so, unable to sin, the breath is regarded as the only sinless thing, because it cannot be overcome by evil. This quality makes it by definition the safest tool to be used skillfully in our quest for The Self.

The natural outcome of the equation of *breathing* with *The Self* would be, therefore, to try to control breath in the attempt to reach The Self and to reunite with it.

This brings us to the issue of breathing techniques. Such, are too many to count, and their perusal will exceed the scope of this book. The interested reader is kindly advised to acquaint himself with the subject from external sources, readily available. A prominent breathing system will be mentioned in short, though—the notion of controlling the breath known by its Sanskrit appellation *pranayama,* used in the Hindu and Buddhist spiritual schools and yoga techniques. The term covers many techniques of breath control, which are said to enhance the mind and the spirit, and many, if not all, of the bodily physiological aspects. They are also used, of course, for the personal spiritual advancement. The techniques involve the manipulation and the control of the phases of breathing—the inhalation and exhalation of air, and its retention, in different modes.

We can see, therefore, that breathing is used extensively—for preparatory goals in the spiritual practice as well as for healing. Here, it will be brought in its preparatory capacity.

Let us start with a perusal of what is breathing and how the body does it.

The average person has an arrhythmic, and, for that matter, an uncontrolled breath. He is subject to various physical and mental circumstances, which change rapidly and randomly. Calm at the moment, we can be enraged and stressed the next minute. The breath follows suit, fast and shallow. Then, we hear a joke or meet a friend and we calm down again, bringing the breath to a slower rhythm and deeper amplitude. The faster the thoughts run in our head, the faster we breathe, the slower the thoughts, the slower we breathe.

When we are excited, stressed or nervous, or angry, when the thoughts of "What will be" and "How will I do it" or "Will I succeed" overcome us with their urgent nature, the breath is shallow; as a result, to supply the steady amount of necessary air, its pace is accelerated. Relaxing, brings the breath to a slower pace because of a deeper breathing. There is an interrelation between the two: The mental state conditions the rhythm and the depth of the breath and the breathing is conditioning the body rhythms in all their forms, from heart-beats to brain waves: When it is slower, the body rhythms are slowed also and vice versa.

In contrast, by the very fact that his body is trained to a controlled and disciplined regime, even a modest one, a meditating person has most of the time and circumstances of his life a more even and regulated breathing, slower and deeper. His breath, controlled as well as uncontrolled, is more profound and has a more even rhythm, which at once attests to more relaxed bodily functions.

Slowing the pace of breathing slows in turn the pace of thoughts, not only during the meditation session, but in the daily life, too. The mind can be trained and conditioned; it can be reined and tamed into any state, which for us, as humans, is a behavioral change.

When meditating in a free mode of uncontrolled breath, the pace of our breathing slows naturally and quite appreciably and the pace of the thought flow is slowed also; thus, we attain a more peaceful state of mind and body. However, by controlling the breathing, we are able to control the pace of the flow of thoughts faster and more efficiently, and consciously, and this is important, because it puts us in control of ourselves and so we are not acting instinctively, blindly. Doing this, during the meditation session we are able to attain one of the major goals of meditation, putting a stop to the thoughts, even if only for brief periods.

After a period of constant meditating, which can be shorter or longer—weeks or months, depending on the effort invested and the personal predisposition, the body is channeled into a considerably more regular breathing pattern, one that is rhythmic and much less prone to be affected by external stimuli. Being much less agitated than in the daily life, the thoughts are less erratic and more paced and, in turn, the breath is calmer. There is also a relative measure of control acquired over the bodily functions through the controlled breath.

So how do we breathe while meditating?

We can breathe, of course, as we do normally, without any controlling technique, and this will do. Soon, the breath will be rhythmic and deeper because we are just calmer and more attentive to ourselves than usual. However, we can do better. A more efficient breathing is achieved by changing the usual manner in which we do it.

The average person breathes through the mouth and into the chest. To make it more efficient, one should breathe always through the nose and into the bottom of the lungs. This type of breathing is called *"Diaphragmatic Breathing"*.

Two questions arise in this regard: Why breathing through the nose and why into the bottom of the lungs?

The advice to breathe through the nose is based on three reasons; I shall explain them together with a short perusal of the functioning and of the structure of the breath and of the lungs, where the inhaled air is stored.

The first reason is hidden in the mechanism of breathing. Though the pattern in which the average person is breathing is through the mouth, air is induced through the nose also, simply because the nostrils are always open, presenting a channel permanently available to conduct the air into the body. However, the nostrils are not participating in the process both at the same time and evenly. In providing this wide-open channel for breathing, they alternate in a cycle of between two and four hours each, in which one nostril is dominant and the other is less active, resting, and inversely. For a healthy person, the cycle is even and regulated, but for a person with problems of the respiratory system, the cycle is changed and the participating period of each nostril is shortened or prolonged, depending on the problem. In this regard, breathing through the nose, then, will be good on two accounts. First, to follow consciously the natural cycle of breathing, and, second, to provide a means of physiotherapy to the nasal respiratory path, forcing the blocked nostril, in case of a disorder, to conduct more air into the lungs, even in a small amount. This will assist in the process of healing that the body is providing for itself through its immune system. Through this natural physiotherapy, a balanced breath is achieved, at least in a certain measure, with normal interval periods of nasal breathing.

The second reason for recommending permanent nasal breathing is the influence that it has on the function of the brain. During their activation through breathing, the facial and nasal nerves affect the brain more than oral breathing. Functioning in an orderly and rhythmic manner, they, in turn, stimulate the brain's hemispheres (and other parts of the brain) more efficiently. It does so in an alternative manner: the right nostril affects the left hemisphere, and vice-versa, thus having a synchronizing and regulating influence on them, able to diminish, or even eradicate, an erratic predominance of one hemisphere of the brain over the other.

The last, and third reason for a nasal breathing, lies in the physical qualities of the air after its passage through the nose: It is cleaner than the air induced through the mouth, warmer and humidified.

It is cleaner because it passes through the hair screen found at the front end of the nose, inside the nostrils. Compared to the mouth, the nose provides a longer path to the air passing through the nostrils into the lungs, warming it more than the mouth is able. The mucus in the nose and the longer path humidify the inhaled air, thus preventing the drying of the respiratory path by the air flow.

Now, the second question is why the need to breathe into the bottom of the lungs, giving it the appellation "diaphragm, or diaphragmatic breathing". The answer for this is simple and it has to do with the efficiency of breathing.

The average person breathes into the upper part of the lungs, better known as breathing into the chest, or worse, into the upper chest, as is the case with most women. In better instances, some breathe into the middle of the lungs, better known as breathing into the upper abdomen. In these kinds of breathing, the inhaled air is stored into the upper third of the lungs or in its two upper thirds, providing the body with a smaller quantity of oxygen than could be provided if the lungs were filled to their full capacity. To compensate for the smaller quantity of air and, therefore, of oxygen contained in each breath, the respiration becomes more frequent; in turn, the respiration is shallower, since one cannot breathe in a rapid pace fully and deeply.

By breathing fully, or "into the diaphragm", we simply follow consciously the contraction and expansion movements of the diaphragm in the process of breathing. The diaphragm is a muscle situated just beneath the lungs. When we inhale, the air fills the lungs and in the process they push the diaphragm, contracting it; it does so in a proportionate relation to the quantity of air inhaled—more air in, more contracted the diaphragm is, less air in, less contracted it is. When we stop inhaling, the ongoing pressure on the diaphragm diminishes and it starts to expand. In doing so, it presses the lungs, and the exhalation part of the breathing process begins.

From the explanation above, it is clear that when we breathe into the bottom of the lungs or, so to speak, "into the diaphragm", instead of "into the chest" or "into the (upper) abdomen", we simply fill the lungs with air more than if we breathe in a shallower manner. By doing so, the accessible volume of the lungs for the incoming air, the inhaled air, is bigger and more air is inhaled. If more air is brought into the body, then more oxygen is made available to it in direct proportion.

To see what type of "breather" you are, look at your chest and abdomen, or, better, put one hand on your chest and the other on your stomach and notice in what part of the lungs the air goes mainly, by following the movement of the hands upwards when the lungs are filled. The one that moves up denotes where the air went, into the chest or into the upper abdomen. Then, start inhaling in a *diaphragmatic* fashion: Put your hand over this region, on the lower abdomen, and ensure that when you breathe, it raises. If it rose, then you brought the inhaled air into the bottom of the lungs, pushing the diaphragm fully, most efficiently. You breathed diaphragmatically. Try to make it a habit in all your activities, literally—walking, sleeping, doing sport, everything.

There is more to it, though. To make it a "*Complete Diaphragmatic Breathing*", not just *Diaphragmatic*, the inhalation phase should be done to the point in which the shoulders are rising appreciably. They rise anyway during inhalation, because the lungs push them upwards, just as they push the diaphragm down and the surrounding rib cage to all sides, however, inhaling as much as you can raises the shoulders maximally; then, a maximal quantity of air is inhaled. To see and feel the difference between a simple *Diaphragmatic Breathing* and a *Complete Diaphragmatic Breathing*, breathe into the bottom of the lungs and then continue breathing until the shoulders rise the farthest. Breathing in this manner fills the lungs to their utmost capacity, supplying the body with the greatest amount of oxygen.

There is an added advantage to it. In so doing, all the internal organs and inner walls of the body surrounding the lungs are massaged continually and rhythmically, a good thing.

It also increases the inhaled quantity of a certain type of energy—*prana* (for this important term see, please, the relevant section in Chapter Seven), yet another advantage.

To sum it up, there are roughly five types of breathing and so, five types of breathers: the upper chest breathing, the chest breathing, the abdomen breathing, the bottom-of-the-abdomen or the diaphragmatic-breathing and the complete-diaphragmatic-breathing. The most efficient, and so, the most advantageous type, is the complete-diaphragmatic-breathing.

After this rather prolonged discussion on breathing, the advantages of a nasal and diaphragmatic breathing are obvious. It improves breathing in all its aspects. It increases the input quantity of oxygen and prana to the body. It provides a cleaner, warmer and more humid air to the lungs, and so, to the body. It improves the cyclic nasal breathing pattern, balancing and synchronizing the brain hemispheres through their rhythmical stimulation. Last, but not least, it massages our internal organs and the inner body linings.

Summary

A proper meditational environment will provide a more efficient meditation. For such an environment, it will be best to choose a time and place that will affect us as little as possible. The predawn hours are the best, and a secluded and permanent consecrated place is recommendable. Our clothes should be light and comfortable. The lotus or the half-lotus posture are the original ones, but sitting or lying are better for the reasons described. If we adopt the sitting position, then we sit erect, though not rigidly so, forming a straight line between the spine and the neck, with closed eyes and mouth, as a rule. A nasal breathing should be adopted, fully done and into the bottom of the lungs.

Chapter Six

The H of M – How to Meditate?

. . .

Systems of Meditation and Techniques employed

In perusing the techniques employed in the meditation process, I shall follow the explanation given for it in Ch. Four, therefore, the subject will be presented here in the same order and will use the same definitions—Relaxation, Concentration, Meditation, Contemplation and, optional, Adoration.

Before we proceed further, however, regarding the use of terms in detailing the meditation process and its parts, a much needed explanation and clarification is necessary.

The terms *concentration*, *breathing* and *meditation*, and, in the more recent times, even the *relaxation* term, are used invariably in a manner that creates a confusing mix. This mix leads the uninitiated person to believe that each of these terms or a partial, random combination of them, can be perceived as *meditation* per se, or intended as tools to be used concurrently while meditating.

Strictly discussing the subject of meditation, and certainly in the manner in which it is approached in this book, none of these two kinds of presenting these terms is correct, and in so doing, a gross misperception of the subject is put forth.

The starting point to clarify this misperception is the classification of the meditation process detailed in Ch. Four.

As explained, concentration and meditation are two distinct parts, stages or phases of the meditation process as a **whole**. Breathing and concentration are auxiliary means in this practice, to be used as a tool and a preliminary stage, respectively, to the meditation stage itself, and as continuous supporting tools thereafter, in the contemplation stage.

Breathing, as a useful tool, is used through all the meditation routine, from the relaxation stage to the contemplation and on to adoration - if one chooses to perform it - but in a very specific manner, one that is *minor* to the one employed in the great breathing techniques (which the reader is invited to explore separately).

In spirituality, breathing is used in two fashions—as a relaxing and self-disciplining tool in the process of meditation, which, in terms of intensity and structure, is the minor use, so to speak, and as a yoga practice means to facilitate cleansing, purification, healing and spiritual advancement – which, in terms of intensity and structure, is its major use.

What is widely known in public about breathing and its place in the spiritual practice is the use that the yoga schools make of it. What is not so widely known is the use that can be made of it in the practice of meditation when applied properly, as a disciplining and taming force, facilitating the first necessary stage of relaxation and the ensuing, equally necessary stage of concentration. Then, maintained and continued together with the concentration achieved, breathing is continuously supporting the next three stages – meditation, contemplation and adoration.

Given that meditation is a tool, albeit a most powerful one, in the advance toward a profound spirituality besides many others, like *purification*, proper *nutrition*, proper *conduct* and proper *thought*, the use of the tool of breathing should be adapted to it as necessary.

The most important criterion in the adaptation of

breathing to the needs of meditation is that the overall and ultimate aim of meditation should take precedence, and this means that everything contradictory to the goal of being unified with the Universal Self while emptying oneself of his own consciousness should be avoided and discarded. The practice of an intricate method of breathing during meditation will stand in the way of being disconnected from oneself and then unified with the All, the Universal, because it requires a dual type of concentration—it requires that the meditator will concentrate on the goal of meditation and on the breathing at the same time. Doing so distracts him from being in a state of union, of fusion, if you will, with the Universal, losing himself in the process, erasing, eradicating really, any existing duality.

As mentioned, such intricate methods of breathing find their justified use in whole in the yoga systems that list them in their inventory of tools, besides many others.

During the meditation routine, a different method of breathing is required, less intense and less structured, a method that helps the meditator to relax and then, to concentrate. Further, when he is concentrated enough, he needs to be able to meditate in the fundamental meaning of the word, thinking lucidly and profoundly, intensely and very analytically, about something. Then, he proceeds to the contemplation phase, and then, further on yet, to the adoration stage, if he so wishes. In these last three stages, the breathing should be of a helpful nature, not distracting the meditator from, nor interfering with, the process. Such type of breathing can be found only in the natural kind that we breathe usually, as an involuntary physical activity.

To sum up this explanatory discussion about breathing in the process of meditation per se, only the moderate, unstructured type of breathing, the natural kind, should be used as a continuous underlining means of support for the maintenance of the whole process of meditation through all its stages and through all its duration. This, in contrast with the more complicated, very structured, methods of breathing that are used in the various schools of spirituality, and indeed, in all schools of yoga, with great success.

Following breathing and accompanying it as an auxiliary tool, concentration is used from the end of the attainment of relaxation to the very end of the **whole** meditation process, maintained scrupulously throughout the practice of the stages of meditation, contemplation and adoration. It should not be confused with the meditation stage itself. As stated, it is only a tool used to maintain a successful meditation, preceding it and continued, while doing it, as a supporting underlining tool for its practice.

During the concentration stage, all that is perceived and accomplished is a deep sense of being focused. We are not yet at the stage of meditation itself, only at its gates. Once we feel concentrated enough, we can start the meditation stage. From this point on, the concentration attained is to be maintained and continued through the remaining parts of the whole meditation routine, the subsequent stages of contemplation and adoration.

Following this much needed explanation and clarification, we shall meet, first, techniques that enable us to relax and, in so doing, to implement the stage of *Relaxation*. Then, we shall discuss techniques that will facilitate a more efficient concentration for the *Concentration* stage and for the rest of the process of meditation. Finally, the stages of *Meditation, Contemplation* and *Adoration* will be presented in detail.

Relaxation Techniques

As stated in Ch. Three, in the explanation for the Relaxation stage, to be able to concentrate fully and in a greater measure of success, we have to be relaxed, we have to be in a state of bodily and mental calmness.

Relaxation, by definition, means the opposite of *stress* and *tension*. Stress and tension is a common human experience. Through the process of relaxation, this stress is removed, or greatly reduced, and with it, the related symptoms in the body and in the mind. In the body, we reduce the stiff tonus of the muscles resulting from such stress; in the brain, our organism releases various kinds of tranquilizers and mood enhancers. As an immediate result, on the physical level, the heart rate, the blood pressure and the metabolism rate decrease in direct proportion to the measure of stress relieved. On the mental level, we feel relieved and more comfortable and contented with the situation.

There are many techniques to achieve relaxation for its

own sake. Based on their easiness and immediacy, only a few will be presented here, to be applied to the meditation process. For more techniques, any good article or book on the subject can be consulted. You may also use other methods, which you know or find, of course.

The relevant relaxation techniques can be categorized in three classes.

Muscle affecting techniques—a direct attempt to release the tension in the muscles, expressed by a stiff tonus, by exercising, or focusing on them in a certain manner.

Breathing—the use of our breath to decrease the level of anxiety induced by the stress we experience.

Visualization—a deliberate attempt to envision ourselves in situations and places that have a calming influence on us.

After a while, as it is with any repetitive activity, relaxing through any method becomes a conditioned reflex, and the meditator is relaxed almost immediately upon positioning himself for the meditation session.

Muscle affecting techniques

Progressive Relaxation

Otherwise known as the Jacobson Relaxation technique, after the name of its founder, Dr. Edmund Jacobson, it consists of first tensing and then relaxing the muscles in an ordered sequence, always starting and ending in the same points. My advice is to start from the top to bottom, which means from the neck and the shoulders, through the arms and hands, then the back and the chest, the abdomen, the thighs and the buttocks, and finally, the legs and the feet.

Obviously, this is performed in the sitting or lying down positions; the lotus postures are unfit for this type of relaxation, the body being too contorted for it.

We start by observing and focusing on the tension in the muscles, or the lack of it. Since we start with the neck, in the beginning we observe the muscles there and focus our attention on them. We tense the muscles and release them. The tension is held for about five seconds, and then we release it and relax for about thirty seconds. Then, we proceed to the next muscle in the group, the shoulders. Finishing with this group, we go to the next, and so on, ending with the feet.

While doing it, we notice the feeling of tension and relaxation and the contrast between them, trying to be aware of it.

The process may seem tedious at first, but it is worthwhile doing, at least in the first days or weeks of meditating. It should take a few minutes, only.

During the process, we can feel how the muscles are loose, muscle after muscle, group after group, having lost their stiffness. Reaching the end, we are relaxed.

Release-only Relaxation

In this technique, the relaxation is achieved also by releasing the tension present in the muscles, but, unlike the Progressive Relaxation technique, it does not employ the building of intentional tension prior to releasing it.

The technique is simple, indeed. After reaching an even breathing rhythm, we focus on the release of any tension present in the muscle groups as mentioned in the Progressive Relaxation technique. The process is continued until a complete feeling of relaxation is achieved.

Breathing Relaxation Techniques

As mentioned in the previous chapter, the average person breathes in the chest. This is especially true when we are stressed. In this case, as mentioned before, the breath is shallow and rapid. To relieve the tension, the diaphragmatic breathing is recommended (see, please, "Breathing" section in former chapter).

Let us see how relaxation through breathing works in the sitting meditation position.

Try to determine, first, what type of breather you are (again, please see "Breathing" in former chapter).

Inhale and exhale through your nose and as deep as you can "into the diaphragm", thus bringing the air into the bottom of the lungs. For the first sessions of meditation look at the abdomen and observe its expanding and contracting movements. This will enable you to do it consciously, fully aware of it. If you wish to feel it and so to make yourself even more aware of it, put one palm over the abdomen and observe its movements—it will follow the movements of the abdomen.

In this initial phase, just follow the natural cycle of your breathing and its way in and out of the body during the inhaling and exhaling stages.

All we have to do to relax in this manner is to breathe in our natural rhythm, but, again, try to do it in a nasal and diaphragmatic fashion. After a while, the breath is slower and deeper, slowing down with it all the other bodily functions, relieving the tensions in the body. Tranquility came upon us and we are relaxed.

Besides the meditation use, this technique can be used as a ready-made and available means for relaxation at any time and in any place.

Visualization

Visualization, or *Guided Imagery,* is a process during which we envision ourselves in positive and comfortable, pleasant situations. This has a decidedly soothing influence on us.

In what seems to be a repetitive and, maybe, a redundant approach, visualization is performed best when we are lightly relaxed, just in the measure to enable us to perform it undistracted. This apparent inner contradiction is in full accord with the entire loose approach to all the aspects of the meditation process that I uphold, from the following of its stages to the choosing and the use of any means of doing it. In this case, we mingle and overlap two different means for the same goal. Being relaxed just a little, we can focus better on the visualization process. But why, you might ask. Relaxation is exactly the purpose for which we do the visualization, so why do I need to visualize if I am already relaxed? Saying that relaxation is needed in order to perform visualization, is to say, essentially, that visualization is unnecessary for relaxation.

This is an "optical illusion": Visualization is a potent means to attain relaxation, so it is worthwhile to relax a little beforehand in order to gain full relaxation in the end.

The relaxation necessary for visualization is superficial;

we seek a light relaxation. Then, when we are relaxed in a basic measure, we start the visualization.

The simplest way to achieve a light relaxation is to focus for a while on our breathing cycle, the inhalation and the exhalation phases. Now, relaxed, we can start the visualization.

Visualizing means exactly what it says, to imagine something, to give it visual perception. In this case, we imagine that we are in situations and places that are pleasant and congenial.

These circumstances can be situations in which we were involved in real life or situations that are conjured by us, imaginary ones, completely made up; such can be a readjustment of something that happened already or just pure imagination, daydreaming. Let's try it.

You may recall how you sat on the grass in the park near you, the other day, leaning against the trunk of that old oak tree, watching the squirrel leaping around in its funny way, its tail high in the air, quivering. Reliving it, you remember the smile that rose in your heart and in your soul. You are there, savoring every bit of it, calmed, soothed in the peace of the moment. Your heartbeat slows down; the breath is slower and deeper; the body "falls" into its own recesses while the muscles loose their stiff tonus that kept them contracted. You are relaxed.

You can imagine the same scene without it ever happening, all an offspring of your boundless imagination.

You can do even better, imagining yourself in a dreamland, a heavenly peaceful place, so very pleasant. You sit on the grass again, leaning against the same old man tree, the squirrel jumping around, looking for an acorn. This time, a creek is flowing by, sparkles glowing in the sun where the water touches the rocks strewn here and there in the streambed. The trickling sound of the water mingles with the rustle of the leaves of the oak tree in the light breeze. White clouds pass by gently, hanging from the endless blue canopy of the skies, swimming on in an ever-changing pattern, visible through the Spanish moss draping the tree's branches. All is so quiet and peaceful, an eternity embedded in the moment. This little corner of a world of your own absorbs you and you are lost in it. The entire universe is forgotten in an unnoticed abandon. You are soothed. You are relaxed.

Now, after being relaxed, you are ready to start the concentration stage without fear of being distracted by a present state of body and mind. You will also find it easier to fend other, new distractions coming your way.

Concentration Techniques

Let us recapitulate the subject of concentration a little.

Since meditating is really thinking, and since this is what we do in that specific stage of the meditation routine, the need to be already concentrated when we start thinking purposefully about something is obvious. Then, when we focus the mind on that subject, the concentrated state into which we brought ourselves, facilitates it immediately and easily. If we need to start concentrating the mind at the same time when we start thinking, then we are performing the *concentration* stage, not the *meditation*, but in this instance we are doing it unconsciously, blurring the thinking process in the meantime, until we are concentrated enough to think clearly and sharply. So, since it is automatically done to enable a clear and successful thinking, the fact that an effort to concentrate is performed, albeit unconsciously, has to be recognized. Therefore, this natural preparatory part of thinking has to be defined as such and to be performed as such, in and of itself. The practice of a specific stage of concentration provides a better quality to it than concentrating subconsciously.

In principle, the thing to do in order to achieve a satisfactory level of concentration is to focus ourselves intently on one item, solely. The measure of the purposefulness and of the seriousness applied while doing it, will bring an appropriate level of concentration. In other words, the measure of dedication and determination applied, notions mentioned in Chapter Two, is the key to achieve the necessary level of concentration. By the way, the process of concentrating on one thing is termed by many as 'meditation', a perfect example of the confusion surrounding the definition of the meditation term, mentioned in the Chapter Four.

All the myriad of ways mentioned by anyone involved in the pursuit, and serious enough to understand the deep importance and place of concentration in the meditation process, and so, to envisage a means to facilitate it in one way or the other, emphasize one thing: Stand still and do not waver in your attempt to achieve long lasting and deep concentration! In other words, as it is written specifically in the Upanishads, the old Hindu scriptures: "Be steady in the light!"

What is meant by this maxim posted in the beginning of this book, is the basic, ultimate need to remain as much as possible fixed in *one place*, to be glued to it, oblivious to anything else while sitting and being quiet, as the preliminary stage to that of meditation itself. This place is the focus of the mind, to be explained shortly. This steady focus, this conscious and deliberate fixity is carried to the point that anything else is falling into the background, taking a back seat, humming quietly its incessant, worldly tune, but not disturbing the meditator anymore to the point of distraction. When concentrating, this is the desired goal.

This place of focus is the center of the field of vision that we encounter as we sit with our eyes closed, trying to concentrate. As explained before, it extends right in front of our eyes up to an arm's length.

When present, this fixed point is material, having physical properties of which we are very much aware. It appears as lights, called phosphenes, as remembered. They have an appearance of a silvery ball, strongly bright and radiant, a light in the field of vision, flickering wildly in minuscule fragments and sparks, exploding in every direction from its center, mainly, but from other parts in it also. It is born anew at random every few seconds, an ever renascent luminous focus, taking an endless range of amorphous shapes. It grows steadily, and then, it disappears gradually but quite fast, dispersing in the field of vision in amorphous, luminescent sparks and shapes. Following suit, another luminous little spark appears in its place, growing again, as the previous one did just seconds before, and so on, again and again, in a seemingly endless silvery balls parade. This succession of lights, of silvery balls, goes on until, suddenly, we lose it. It may come again of its own accord, or it has to be made anew by our consciously concentrated effort. This confirms fully the necessity of the maxim "Be steady in the light". An explanation for these lights has been presented in Chapter Two, in the section "Signs of finding and reuniting with the Self".

To keep the concentration on, we have to be focused steadily on this volcanic, erupting center of field of vision, a hand unshaken holding the candle, the inner eye of an attention that does not falter. If we maintain a stable hold on it, in a short time we shall witness its rebirth from the same center, the same place in which it sparkled and into which it disappeared a moment ago. In the same time, we experience a profound measure of concentration, a robotic almost, steely inner core that enables us to make and to sustain this effort. We may not be aware of it at the time, but there it is: We were concentrated to the utmost. This maximum measure of concentration is accompanied sometimes by a distinct sense of disconnection, as explained before in the term "sensory depravation".

Six techniques of facilitating concentration will be presented here. They are the *OM Repetition* and *OM Repetition Plus, Mind Focus* and *Mind Focus Plus, OM Focus Plus* and *Super-Focus Power Repetition*. The first two techniques are based on repetition, the next three on focusing, and the last one on tapping a certain energy in us in a combination of focusing and repetition. The "plus" term means, of course, that the method is the same as the former but enhanced.

The *OM Repetition Plus, OM Focus Plus* and *Super-Focus Power Repetition* are methods that I developed in the course, and as a result, of many years of meditating. They appear here, publicly, for the first time.

Experiencing them, you will find that they are quite simple and easy to perform, yet powerful.

OM Repetition

Before we go on with the presentation of this routine, a basic explanation of the terms "*OM*" and "*mantra*" is in order.

OM is a principal mantra in the performance of the Hindu and Buddhist practices, sacred and the most venerated of them all. *Mantra* is an incantation repeated to enhance the spiritual experience. It can be a sound, a word, a sentence or some other complex expression.

OM is perceived as an efficient tool that can bring the Seeker to the point of crossing the gate between the worldly matter and The Self, helping to attain it. As a tool, it is used as a single-term mantra, or with other words or sounds, forming a composite mantra, usually as the first in the compound.

When uttered, it is heard as the articulation of the vowels 'a' as in "ah", 'u' as in "foot" and the consonant 'm'—the combination 'AUM', in close continuation. Uttered, it is sustained as a hum, as if the sound of 'm' is continued as long as possible. Note that those sounds are made first in the centre of the palate, when uttering the 'a', then, the sound reverts to the back of the palate, when uttering the 'u', and, finally, between the closed lips, when uttering the 'm'. Then, the sound of 'm' is prolonged as a nasal hum. Also note that in all this sequence, the mouth is open for the utterance of 'a', half-open for 'u', and closed for 'm'.

This order of incantation of the three sounds is suggestive of the ancient Indian notion of comparing the exalted nature of the mantra OM, in its ability to advance the seeker on the path of spirituality toward the Self, to a bird, the high soaring white goose. The seeker sits, as it is, on its tail—A, in the middle of the bird's body between its wings—U and M respectively. Having gotten hold of the two wings, seated firmly on the bird, he soars to higher levels, finding the Self and reposing on it.

The OM repetition technique toward facilitating concentration is simple—repeating the mantra until the proper level of concentration is achieved. The mantra can be repeated aloud or silently. When I meditate using this concentration technique, I do it silently; only rarely I do it aloud. This is so, because I employ this mantra as a means to concentrate, not as a means in itself, which is practiced also, and so, I find it distracting to the concentration effort to utter it aloud.

For obvious reasons, the repetition occurs during the exhaling cycle of breathing—you cannot possibly utter something coherently while inhaling. You will find that this is so even when expressing it silently—it is easier to do it during exhalation even when not voicing it.

OM Repetition Plus

This technique makes use of the mantra OM in combination with the *Complete Diaphragmatic Breathing*. In doing so, besides increased concentration, we gain all the advantages mentioned in the Breathing section of Ch. Five—increased quantities of oxygen and prana, and massage of the internal organs.

In this technique we recite the mantra 'OM' while breathing in the complete diaphragmatic breathing manner. In the same time, we try to be aware of the prana intake and to channel it to the pineal and pituitary glands in the brain (please read the relevant sections, Prana and Head, in Chapter Seven). The channeling is done by using the imagination, visualizing bringing the prana from the crown chakra to the glands.

Mind Focus

In this technique, the object of our attention is the center of the field of view during meditation when we do it with closed eyes.

All we do is staring at it steadily for an extended time. After a while, depending on the level of relaxation attained in the previous stage, a satisfying level of concentration is achieved. We are concentrated now, and are able to proceed to the next step, the meditation stage.

Mind Focus Plus

As the name implies, we do the Mind Focus technique with a certain addition, which is the manipulation of the lights seen when concentrating.

We have talked already about phosphenes, the sparks of light of all shapes and sizes that jump in the field of view, mainly in its center.

As explained already, if we persist in staring at this light steadily, unhesitatingly, it changes gradually, but quickly, into a silvery ball, into which all the other individual sparks converge, leaving the rest of the field of view black.

At this exact moment, not before and not after it, move the ball from the center of the field of view to the *crown chakra* (for a detailed explanation of the term, see, please, the Chakras section in Chapter Seven). This chakra is located on the top of the skull, in the center of it. The ball is moved by visualization or by "taking and dragging" it swiftly with the eyes, acting as the "hand" that holds it.

In both instances, the movement and the positioning of the light ball in that chakra is accompanied by a strong, tickling and pleasant, physical feeling in the whole neck and the rear end of the mouth, though more so when done with the eyes, probably because of the muscular movements. Together with this feeling, there is a strong mental sense of concentration and fulfillment, almost to the point of an orgasmic physical excitement, in the whole head, from the neck to the top of the skull.

The ball should be moved at the exact moment of its full formation, not before and not after it, because only in this moment it is fully made and so potent in causing the strong sense of concentration wanted. Moreover, if it is done untimely, there is a distinct sense of lack of completion of task, therefore you will know if you did it timely or not.

This technique can be done once, if we feel satisfied with the level of concentration gained, or repeatedly, until we feel that we are concentrated enough to proceed further.

The concentration achieved is steady and strong, enabling us to go comfortably to the next stage, the meditation part of the session.

OM Focus Plus

This technique is a combination of the *OM Repetition Plus* and *Mind Focus Plus* techniques.

All the activities in this technique are performed in the same time. We focus our attention in the *center* of the field of view, recite the *OM* mantra, are attentive to the *prana* absorbed and channel it to the *pineal* and *pituitary glands* in the brain, and drag the *silvery ball of light* that appears in the center of the field of view to the *crown chakra.*

This technique is quite complex but very efficient when performed fully and correctly.

Super Focus Power Repetition

This technique employs another complex activity in an attempt to attain strong concentration.

Here we shall tap the energetic centers of our body, the *chakras,* channeling the energy found in the lowest one, the *kundalini,* to the most elevated, the *crown chakra,* and we shall activate the spiritual centers, the *pineal* and the *pituitary* glands. As you shall see, this technique is very potent. It induces sharp concentration and triggers strong physical sensations. Again, before reading further, please be acquainted with the chakras system as detailed in the Chakras section in Chapter Seven.

Sitting in the meditation posture, visualizing the activity, we "look" at the chakras from the one in the space above the head, to the one beneath our feet, in the earth, nine chakras, in total. We do so by turning our attention to them and visualizing them for a moment, not more, from the chakra located a few inches above the head, and then to the next one, the crown chakra, and so on, until we reach the chakra beneath our feet, in the earth, embedded a few inches there. This should take less than a minute, not more, as a reminder of their presence, sight and location.

Reaching the last chakra, after "seeing" it there, we start to visualize it rotating clockwise for a few seconds. Doing the same, we then go to the next, the root chakra or the kundalini, and so on, ending with the chakra above the head.

You can do all this in any pace comfortable for you. I look at the chakras in a natural pace, one after another, and then, when I start rotating them, I do it during the exhalation phase of the breathing. During the inhalation phase, I direct my attention to the next chakra and focus on it; when I start to exhale, I rotate it.

Upon finishing this part of the performance, we direct our attention to the root or kundalini chakra. Focusing on it, we contract the muscles at the end of the spine, surrounding the coccyx bone, the place of the root chakra. This, naturally, will cause the contraction of the anal sphincter muscle in some measure also, but the emphasis is on the region of the end of the spine.

Upon contracting, a rush of some kind will be sensed, something that can be defined as a charge of energy, rolling and tumbling up the spine into the base of the head and into the head, into the brain. A strong, almost orgasmic physical excitement is felt then, reeling us into a tremor through the upper body, and the head especially, a tremor that can be rather strong. This experience can be so strong that some cry instantly, moved to tears by this sudden flush of energy up the spine and into the head.

Now, that the main energetic centers of the body are activated and we directed the kundalini energy into the head, we turn our attention to the pineal and pituitary glands. The aim is to activate them, also. To do so, we caress them, or rub them gently.

Visualizing the glands (again, please read the section on Head in Chapter Seven), we imagine rubbing them lightly with the thumb and the index fingers, caressing them both at the same time, back and forth.

The concentration achieved in this technique is more than just being concentrated, it is a sharp feeling of encounter with our body from head to toe, an awareness of being in the body and of acknowledging it in its absolute presence in the here and now. A totality of unity of our body and our consciousness is achieved, one that would not be gained otherwise in such a pronounced measure.

Those techniques are only a few of many others that can be employed to achieve a satisfactory level of concentration. The important thing is to achieve it, and to achieve it in a manner that is comfortable to you, and so, to go forth to the next stage, the meditation stage, there to reflect, to think about anything you want, anything you like, anything at all. There we go now.

Meditation

We know, now, that when we speak about *meditation,* we mean the *reflective thinking process* and the specific stage in the *meditating session* in which it is undertaken, not the complete meditation course. What we need to mull over, though, is what can possibly be suitable subjects for thinking and if we want to achieve something doing it, and if yes, what.

Considering the question of what is suitable for thinking akin to putting limits on it, it would be unacceptable at the personal level to do so, for we do not deal with the question of what is suitable to think from a technical point of view but from a thematic one, therefore, we touch on ethics here. Freedom of thought should be, and is, unquestionable. From a technical point of view, this is not a problem, we just think—we can do it anywhere, anytime, in any position; the thematic point of view is what makes it worthy of discussion. Being aware of the freedom of thought that anyone should enjoy as a fundamental right, the question is still there, nevertheless: Is it all right to continue thinking about everything that pops up in our head? Thoughts make deeds and this is the catch.

Thoughts and fragments of thoughts pop up in our head all the time; it is up to us to follow them in further systematic thinking or to disregard them entirely. After all, thoughts are the basis of future action, the abstract outline that is put into a frame of real, tangible factors when the decision is taken to transform them into reality. They are the blueprint for the initial phase in their full material implementation, something that a man of action worth his salt perceives as the final phase of the project he entertains—its completion. If this is so, then maybe we should not entertain *any* thought. It may turn into reality, and if the thought was *incorrect* according to the Law of Universal Love, then, on a mundane level, the ensuing action, turned into reality, would be of a negative nature, contrary to the endless, unconditional and unselfish kind of love that rules the Creation. Negative thoughts may lead to negative actions—demeaning, trespassing, or outlandish behavior, use of narcotics, violent and vicious sex, murder, war; all of that and more are incorrect according to the Law of Universal Love. The negative thoughts turned into negative actions will also bring negative karma.

Yet thoughts are unruly creatures, wild and erratic, with very little matching controlling ability on our part. In spite of our best efforts, they pop up out of nowhere in the most surprising times, dealing with the most surprising subjects.

In this stage, though, the meditation stage, it is not our goal to eliminate them, since this is not the place and time to apply non-thinking techniques (to be dealt with in the next section, Contemplation), as what we are doing is exactly this, thinking.

Here, it is important to mention that we need to be careful with what we say, because we can plant what can be called seed-thoughts in another's mind, with which he may not be able to deal properly and so can lead to negative acts.

Back on track, since we are now in the thinking stage and we do not want to eliminate thoughts, we need to seek a remedy to the real possibility of the particular action-reaction chain, the potential corresponding negative factual outcome to the initial incorrect, or negative thought.

There are three such remedies, but none can guarantee total success because of the erratic nature of the thoughts and because of our human nature and its accompanying feelings.

One can only hope to reach, while entrapped as human in this worldly matter, a point that is as close as possible to the angelic state, in which evolved entities are totally engrossed in an absolute love and this love is embedded in them entirely.

One remedy is to try in earnest, as is the rule with everything we do in this quest, to think *positive* thoughts. If done determinedly, it will turn in time into a habit that may have the upper hand most of the time. I do think that it is impossible for us, humans, to attain a stage in which such thoughts are eradicated entirely from our awareness; nevertheless, we should try tirelessly.

The second remedy is the adoption of the non-attachment attitudinal approach to all kinds of thought, but in particular to the negative ones. This approach calls for a detached attitude on our part, putting a temperate and cool-headed distance between our thoughts and us. All we have to do is to "look at them" in an impersonal manner, observing them dispassionately from afar and from a higher observation point as if they were in the valley below and we on the top of the hill, looking at it. Calmly, non-judgmental and not comparing, putting our feelings at rest, like pouring oil on troubled waters, we stare at them as they appear and as they change into other, sometimes entirely different thoughts, in a seemingly endless parade of uncontrollable creatures of the conscious and the subconscious mind. Presently, they will disappear; others will come and take their place, but, in time, by and by, with determination and loving patience for ourselves, there will be fewer and our rate of success in controlling and suppressing them will certainly be higher.

The third remedy is a simple, direct approach: Do not put them into action.

When applied, these three remedies are not to be forced upon ourselves but performed gently, patiently, without any expectation. For our quest, these approaches are positive actions, because they teach us to think and act positively, to act dispassionately, without attachment, and to be disciplined, in not putting certain thoughts into action.

With this in mind, there is a certain positive aspect to a reflective thinking routine, which can be applied to all kinds of thought, positive and negative, upon which we touched in Ch. Three—the *self-knowledge* attained by observing our thoughts. We shall elaborate upon it again, here.

Self-knowledge is maybe the second most important goal and attainment to which we should look when engaged in our quest, following suit the quest for The Self.

Such knowledge is obtainable by analyzing what we see when observing ourselves and what we see when we are mirrored in the activities of *another*, any other person that we may encounter in our march in life.

When it is us that we observe, we do it, obviously, when we are engaged in two permanent practices: thinking our thoughts and performing our activities. Analyzing ourselves, though, in the mirror of our thoughts versus self-analysis through our activities, can be tentative at best, since we cannot be sure that we are objective, that we are indeed what we see. The psyche is playing tricks on us, sometimes, leading us into self-delusion of various forms, while our activities show who we truly are, to the world and to us. Even so, though, with this shortcoming taken into consideration, trying to know ourselves through our thoughts can be quite informative and educative.

Knowing ourselves leads to knowledge of the other and of the world, for our neighbor and the whole world are a replica of us, and vice versa. We are a microcosmic replica of the macrocosm.

"As above, so below!"

Here, we come upon an interesting and seemingly contradictory point regarding the correctness of the thoughts in the light of the Law of Universal Love. In essence, this is the same issue mentioned directly above when dealing with the possible negative outcome of negative thoughts in the real world. Let us present the question and its full implication.

If we are to know ourselves truly and completely, or at least as deep and broad as we can reach into our soul, into our psyche, then will it not be advisable to look at *any* thought that appears, to observe *any* thought that happens to cross our mind? Censoring our thoughts and discarding what is incorrect in the light of the Law of Universal Love is to disregard whole parts of ourselves, thereby omitting readily available opportunities for self-knowledge. This could be a true waste.

If the attempt to know ourselves can be an obstacle to

the fundamental law, then we should seek remedies for this hazard, too. And we have them. They are two of the same remedies to be employed against the negative thoughts while meditating, mentioned above: Use the non-attachment tool in order to discard the negative thoughts and avoid making them part of your attitude, and do not put into action every thought that crosses your mind. This is truly and extremely important: Think about anything and everything, but do not become attached to it and do not put it into practice if it is negative, and so incorrect by The Law of Universal Love.

Contemplation

We have reached the final stage in the regular meditating process, the *Contemplation* stage (to remind, there is one more stage, which is **optional**, the Adoration stage).

This is the most important stage in the meditation process, because, in it, we may find the Self, the goal of the whole endeavor that we undertook when we started the meditation session.

By implication, contemplation means taking something from its natural surroundings and putting it by itself in a separate area in which it is to be treated in itself. This is what we are about to do, to treat a particular object in a particular way.

In the meditation stage, we reached a peak of mental activity, preparing ourselves for the next stage, contemplation. In this stage, we reach a peak of activity in which we touch upon higher levels of human awareness, closer to the spiritual on the matter-spirit spectrum as much as we are able. We turn to a point in which, by observing passively but intently the subject of contemplation, we try to reach a meaning of a transcendental kind through this subject.

This phase in the process is one in which, after exerting our mind on various themes meditating on them, meaning thinking, reflecting on them, we turn to a form of attention that lacks immediate practical form. In this regard, the contemplation stage has a dual meaning, depending on the school in which it is applied. It is akin to some Western schools, in particular, in which the meditation stage is a mental activity and the contemplation is one in which we observe passively a subject. Some Eastern schools take the opposite approach, sometimes, so one can find both approaches in both schools.

In the contemplation stage, we do not think, we observe. But not to think is very difficult, as stated before. Nevertheless, there is a means with which we can defeat the thought plague. A very powerful remedy for the errant, roving and straying, piling thoughts is to "look" at the back of the brain. This place is called *"The Place of Darkness"* in some Eastern spirituality schools. Thoughts are formed in the frontal cortex, in the front part of the brain, so it seems natural to go where they are not formed in order to escape them, and it is interesting to see ancient approaches that employ this fact. This tool is efficient and almost immediate. The "looking", of course, is done with the inner eye, placing our attention thereby.

Now is time to see how the contemplation stage is done.

Ending the meditation stage, we are about to enter a world in which we literally stare with our "inner" eye at something or at the empty field of attention spread before our closed eyes (in 'closed eyes' meditation) and do not think. This empty field of attention can be defined quite accurately as "the void of nothingness" for want of better words. If we choose to observe and contemplate a subject, it can be anything and everything as well as the subject on which we just meditated a moment ago.

So all we do in this stage is "looking" at the subject of our choosing or at the void.

If we stare at the void, paradoxically, we will perceive a vast nothingness, and in the same time, a distinct notion of plenty to which nothing else can compare. It is truly a perplexing contradiction to watch and feel but a very pleasant one, for it plays in front of our eyes with full authenticity. In spite of the empty field in front of us, we have a feeling of fullness of a mental kind, one in which we feel that we know everything, that nothing is unknown and that there are no more questions to ask. There is a distinct feeling of deep satisfaction and content fulfillment. It is something that cannot be mistaken, and you will recognize it immediately when it happens.

This plenty, though, having nothing material to offer but something of pure abstract substance, puts us in a place through which we can become very close to ourselves because there is simply nothing else to which we can direct our attention, so we become attuned to ourselves in a most intimate, natural and smoothly gradual way.

In this climate of passive attention to nothing and of nearness to ourselves, there may be an instance of perfect union between the void to which we constantly stare and us. In this instance, we may perceive our Self; by the sudden transformation of the perception experienced, in this instance we may make the jump from matter into the spiritual, from the earthly to the divine.

If we stare at a subject, abstract or concrete, we shall try to perceive it in a manner that conveys to us the transcendental root of its very existence; we shall try to perceive its very being and making. Trying we will—though we do not know what this means, for we had never been there nor did we understand it with our limited human mind, and though it is probably impossible for us, humans, to attain. Nevertheless, through this particular object of contemplation that we chose, we shall try to fathom the root of the very *Existence* itself, the *primordial egg*, and of the coming into being, the birth of this object and, by implication, the birth of all objects, abstract and concrete, animate and inanimate. In itself, this object is not the key to this not-to-be-understood-humanly perception; it is only a means to an end, a tool that we employ in our quest for the Divine in us, The Self. We try stubbornly, again and again, in every contemplation stage of every meditation session, to open the forever-closed for us, to break the unbreakable, to catch a glimpse of the unseen.

In this persistent attempt to penetrate the impenetrable, there may be, occasionally, an instance of seeing the transcendental and of perfect union between the object of our contemplation and us.

In both cases, those of contemplating a subject or staring at the void, we achieve a state in which we may meet the Self, the very goal of our quest; we may find ourselves, occasionally; we may meet ourselves on a very intimate, unmediated level. Through the union achieved between the object of our contemplation and us, we recognize and perceive something that we did not recognize and perceive before; we understand an ultimate meaning of our being and of the Universe, the All. Ultimately, this is what enlightenment is.

In the case of staring at the void, with nothing to draw our attention, unconsciously and unwittingly we come to a degree of closeness to ourselves never achieved before, a nearness that, in rare moments, is uniting us with our Self and so with The Supreme, Universal Self, the object of our quest.

In the case of staring at a concrete object, we try relentlessly to understand the "being" of this subject, its own Self.

But trying as we may, stubbornly, not giving up, something might break. This can be one of two things: Our mind or the wall of the puzzle that we pursue. More than a few times it will be our mind that will break. But if only once we shall succeed to break the wall that protects the puzzle of the transcendental root of the subject's being, if only once we shall manage to break the gates of the tower in which its own Self resides, we shall comprehend the ultimate, the Supreme, Universal Self. Glimpsing it, we shall grasp our own Self, the Divine in us, the object of our quest.

This result, in both approaches—staring at the void or at an object, is not assured, it is not guaranteed, but if the momentous event happens, the quest was accomplished.

In this instance, as a by-product, we experience enlightenment, and this is really the ultimate achievement, for to perceive the divine in us is to be enlightened.

Here, at this point, the meditation process ends. It may end with a successful result, as when we reach the Divine in us, our Self, achieving enlightenment as a by-product, and it may not, but we try nevertheless to reach it, and we try without any defined wish, without any concretized will. We try all the time, not fearing failure, not giving up. All that is there is a constant recognition of The Self in us and of an attempt to reach it and to reunite with it. We also know what the ultimate goal of the meditation process is, but we do not "want" it. The goal is pursued by us in an impersonal way, without bringing our worldly ego into the equation.

Now, we may consider the process finished and go about our day, but some may continue with the next, optional stage of *adoration*. This is the theme of the next passage.

Adoration

As mentioned, this stage in the meditation process is optional. Though this is not a religious book, it would be appropriate to include it in the meditation process, because some, following their belief, use it as an integral part of it in their attempt to be closer to God. This is a demand of any theistic, or religious school to which the adherents comply. In atheistic spiritual schools, the adoration is addressed to the supreme Self, which is Divine. In other instances, the adoration is addressed to the teacher, as explained elsewhere; sometimes, to both subjects: God or the Divine, and the teacher.

The rationale for this action is the equation of love with wisdom, and, consequently, with knowledge—to love the Supreme is to know Him and vice versa.

Adoration is intended sometimes to predispose the revered entity to favor the person doing it, but mostly it is just that, veneration of a higher, more advanced person—the teacher, or supreme entity—God or the Divine.

The duration of this stage is flexible, as is with all the other stages and it reaches its end when the meditator feels that it is time to finish it.

How is this done? In this stage, the meditator turns his attention to the revered entity in an attempt to show his devotion to it. He also renounces all his actions and the fruits of his actions and offers them to this entity, the subject of his adoration. He pours unfettered love toward its subject, prostrating himself, as it is, at its feet. His heart is full with deep love and veneration.

This will mark the end of the meditation process and session.

Exiting the Meditation Process

Finishing the meditation process, we do not open our eyes and switch our attention immediately to the world around us. This could be a little bit of a shock, because of the sudden change of the focus of our attention. Continuing to sit with closed eyes or as the manner in which we meditated left us at its end, we turn our attention gradually to the surrounding world with its noises and fragrances, its incessant pull at us. Only when we feel that we are completely attuned to it again, we acknowledge it fully. Now, we can get up and go to our businesses.

Troubleshooting

Sometimes, problems appear that hinder a smooth flow of a meditation session.

For example, new thoughts are formed and grow to the point where we, unconsciously, leave the meditation process and are entirely absorbed in them. Or, after a period of time during which we did not meditate, days or weeks, and that can happen, it may be difficult to follow the process and to achieve proper relaxation and tranquility of body, mind and spirit.

Following, are some basic and simple remedies to these obstacles on our way to a proper and pleasant meditation process. These means of bringing ourselves to a state of calmness, from which we can proceed with the meditation process, are based on directing our attention consciously to the physical and energetic spots mentioned.

– Body washing – "Washing" our body can be relaxing and, therefore, conducive to a pleasant meditation process. It is a simple procedure and easily done. With eyes closed, of course, we direct our attention to our body, starting with the feet. There, using visualization, we massage them with love and affection. We then start climbing our body, stopping everywhere and massaging the place—feet, hands, shoulders, stomach, chest, back, neck. On our way, we do the same to the inner organs—intestines, kidneys, diaphragm, pancreas, etc. We also enter every orifice and clean the interior. We finish with washing the head and its orifices—ears, eyes, nose and mouth, and the brain and the spine.

– Chakra focusing – Here, we employ the same technique that uses the chakras, detailed in the "Super Focus Power Repetition" approach in the Concentration section in this chapter. The technique has a soothing effect, easing the meditation performance.

– Breathing – As a last resort, breathing can be used to calm us and bring a relaxed state of mind and body. To soothe a state of restlessness, breathing is quite efficient, as mentioned so many times before. It can be used as a troubleshooter in an unrefined form, meaning that we are just being attentive to our breath, following its flow in and out of the body, so just sit and breathe, follow it entering your body while inhaling and getting out of the body while exhaling. This is the best remedy for calming the mind and the body in the worst state of stress, even. A good example is a pregnant woman giving birth using breathing as a relaxing tool. The hour of birth is an extremely stressing time for those women and if they use it to ease the delivery, then we certainly can use it in states of less stress.

They use a different technique, of course, but the efficiency of breathing to ease mental and physical stress is obvious.

Besides those simple means of basic relaxation and soothing, the more sophisticated relaxation tools described in this chapter can be used also, of course; any other means of which you might think is welcome, too, and you are invited to share them with others and me.

Chapter Seven

Wheels that make the Man go round – the Human Body Structure

...

Our many Bodies and the Energetic Matrix, and other related Things

---

What you see when you look at your body is not what you or, for that matter, all of us, really get or, rather, have. The true structure of the human body is something quite different from what we see with our physical eyes.

There are quite a few schemes around describing the "other", more detailed human bodily structure, from times immemorial. This description presents the complete structure of the human body. The conventional science does not endorse it, of course. The most widely mentioned arrangement, the one that is at the basis of many others, is the scheme that counts three basic parts in the human bodily frame: the man's physical body, the spirit and the human unit, or ego. This is NOT the conventional psychological ego, but what may be more accurately called "the seed", around which the various layers of the body are arranged. This personal ego, the *unit* for some, as mentioned above, is the famous Self, mentioned so much in this book, and the goal of the quest, the theme of this book.

This basic scheme of "body, spirit and unit" is found in the Kabbalah, and, in more detail, and sometimes using other terms, in other occult approaches.

In addition to the body structure system in itself, it is to be understood that, as in any actively functioning system, there is a certain part that activates it, controls and directs its operation—from the physical, through the mind, to the spiritual, what we would call the energy supply hub and the command center.

The different bodies are interconnected, as expected, working in unison and, when the body is fully developed in all its aspects, in perfect synchronization. In others, not so developed, or developed weakly spiritually, the various parts are weaker or stronger than others and work in different rhythms and strengths, in an unsynchronized fashion.

In this chapter, these three major parts of the structure that characterizes us as human beings shall be described and investigated in a schematic manner, just enough to enable us to understand the principles behind the facts and the narration. The anatomy of the human body that will be presented here is the accepted occult point of view of the subject, not recognized by science.

The main difference between the two approaches, occult and scientific, is that the occult sees as material everything and anything, including spirit. We should remember that matter converts to pure energy only when it travels at the velocity of light multiplied by itself, as stated by Einstein in his famous formula, $e = mc^2$, where e is energy, m is matter, and c is the speed of light. As mentioned already throughout the book in various places, those two seemingly opposing antipodes, matter and spirit, are really the two ends of the spectrum of a continuous string of matter that presents a decreased density from the end of matter towards the end of spirit, matter being the densest, spirit the rarest. Science, on the other hand, according to its prevalent paradigm, sees as material and, so important in its approach, worthy to be defined as existent, only what can be observed, weighed and measured by the material man's five senses and his analytical tool, the mind, sometimes via the instruments conceived by him.

Another difference is the energetic bodily matrix that the occult is adamant in counting as one of the layers of the human body, one that science is reluctant even to consider.

Yet another difference is the role that the two approaches give to the command and supervising centers of the human body—the brain and the glands therein and throughout the body. The occult affirms that these glands, in addition to their pure physical functions and their contact with matter, are responsible also for the contact with the higher than pure matter in us and in the universe. In detail, this higher substance is intuition, personal sub-consciousness and consciousness, the collective consciousness of humankind and the cosmic bank of knowledge and principles.

Only very recently, and very gradually, had the scientific establishment come to terms with other planes and dimensions than the purely material in dealing with man and the human body. This is apparent in medicine and other related fields, and in personal counseling. More and more individuals of interest—doctors, nurses and counselors, are willing to give a place of recognition to the spiritual side of healing and recuperating from illnesses and various treatments, and life hardships—prayer, relaxation and meditation, and to try them in a medical environment in real circumstances.

The description of the scheme of the human bodily structural system—the material, the mental and the energetic, and the glands located in the head, will start with a broad account of the human body as the occult sees it. It will continue with the energetic matrix depiction and the head glands, and the role of the head as the ultimate place of convergence for spiritual activities and development will be determined.

Besides those aspects of the human physical structure, the cosmic energy that enables the existence of everything in the universe—*prana,* will be described. Prana was mentioned as a by-product of the advantages of the diaphragmatic breathing and in the concentration technique OM Focus Plus, in the Concentration section in the previous chapter.

Last, but not least, will be presented a short summation of the various benefits that the spiritual life and the best tool for it, the meditation activity, convey to the one pursuing them. Following the benefits, a short résumé of the negative influences of meditation will be brought; they should not be ignored.

The Structure of the Human Body

The human life as perceived by the occult is arranged around a seed that "incarnates" in a human body. From the initial instance of incarnation it then repeats it, "*re*incarnating". An explanation of the reincarnation theories is found in Chapter One in the section "The Journey of The Self".

Following this explanation, the description of the various layers of bodies comprising man will make more sense.

Coming into this world, the seed garbs itself with specific garments, outfits suitable for the task. This can be compared to a diver who would immerse himself into a diving suit that meets the various demands of being under water and high pressure. Or to an astronaut who would don a space suit that fits the demands of being exposed to the extreme conditions of flying at a very high speed and in the outer space and going out of the spaceship to perform various tasks.

Likewise, the human seed of existence dresses in the most suitable mantle for the type of worldly material into which it descends, pure matter, the densest in existence. Moreover, the diver and the astronaut, and, actually all of us, have more than one suit in which we dress ourselves, each an additional layer on the previous one worn. Reckon, as we start to dress, we put on at first the underwear, then, if we plan to go outside just to sit in the yard or to work in the garden, we wear some shorts and a light shirt. If we plan to go shopping or to a movie or a restaurant, we leave the underwear on us, of course, changing the light shirt and the shorts to a more fashionable shirt and a pair of trousers, put on socks and then a pair of shoes; then, maybe a tie, as may be the case. If the weather allows, we go out wearing nothing more, but if it is cold outside, we put on another layer of clothes—a jacket and a scarf, and if it rains, maybe even a raincoat. We may put on a hat, to keep us shaded from the sun or just as a style preference; a watch is a permanent attachment for all, by now. To all this we may add a pair of glasses against the glare of the sun, very important. According to our job, we may have a case in our hand, a necessity in many cases, which may be anything between a plain bag and a briefcase, in which we carry our meal, some documents and some gadgets. We do all this just to go out and face the various weather conditions to which we may be exposed and other circumstances that we may encounter during the different situations that we plan to attend when exiting our original place of dwelling. Same with the diver, same with the astronaut: they wear the most suitable outfit for the planned tasks.

Likewise, the seed of the human existence does the same when parting with its origin, The Supreme One, and goes into the material world—it wears different bodies as garments to fit the worlds in which it finds itself.

The various bodies that the seed wears during the reincarnation – in a more detailed scheme than the "body, spirit, unit" mentioned above – are the *physical* body, the *etheric* body, the *feelings* body, the *mental* body and the *spiritual* body.

The *physical* body is the material entity apparent to our five senses. The *etheric* body serves as an interface matrix for enabling energy from the outside, together with internal energy, to imbue and activate us. The *feelings* body is the layer that deals with sensations, often known and mentioned as the *astral* body. The *mental* body is the part that brings to fruition our intellectual faculties, abstract and concrete, analyzing and processing data.

The various bodies are arranged around the seed, which is The Self, as different suits, as explained. The physical body enables it to function in matter; the etheric body is the energy enabler; the feeling body feels other such bodies in the astral world and facilitates the interactions in that world; the mental body is the thought-machine that produces our thoughts, abstract and concrete, and is able to register other thoughts. These thoughts emanate constantly, able to reverberate from the remotest and most secluded place, even from a sealed cave (remember the anchorites mentioned before?) in the remotest mountain, to the four corners of the universe, to be registered in the cosmic knowledge bank, referred to already in Chapter One. The spiritual body assists in the higher spheres.

All the bodies are made of matter, but starting with the etheric body, each of them is less dense than the previous one, the physical body being the densest.

They are not layered one upon the other, but rather infused within each other. A good description for how they are positioned relatively to each other would be that of a bucket filled with stones, in which sand is poured; the sand will fill, then, the empty spaces between the stones; if, then, water is poured in that bucket, it will fill the space between the grains of sand. Finally, what is visible to the eye is a mix of wet sand and stones, a combination of three different materials. The same with our body and its different components—each of them is mixed inextricably with all the others.

The Chakras

In various places on the surface of the etheric body are energetic centers that receive, and then transmit, energy. These centers are the *chakras*, "wheels" in Sanskrit.

Among other definitions and designations, this well-known term denotes the psycho-energetic centers that are said to exist in our body, and it is this with which I am concerned here.

This is a subject too wide to be covered in this book in detail. Being of such importance, though, and because it is mentioned in different places in this book, it will be worthwhile to elaborate on it slightly.

The chakras are located in many points in the body, not only in the famous seven or eight spots mentioned in any book or article about Eastern philosophy and practices. However, because of their relative significance, those few, known most widely, are the ones that are taken into consideration most.

The chakras are vortices of energy facilitation and of connection to the nervous and glandular systems, located on the surface of the etheric body. They stem from a point of origin in the physical body, in the spine, and extend a few inches out of the body in the shape of a trumpet, the opening of which is facing outside. They are connected to the nervous system in the body and to various glands, in a continuous interaction.

Starting from the lowest and accompanied by their Sanskrit name, the following is the most accepted list of them, but by no means the only one.

The first is the "*root*" chakra (*muladhara*, known also as the *kundalini* chakra), located at the base of the spine; some say in the anus. The second, the reproductive system, or the *genital* organs chakra (*svadhishtana*), is located just above the sex organs region. Third, the *navel* chakra (*manipura*), is located at the navel, over the solar plexus. Fourth, is the *heart* chakra (*anahata*), located over the heart. The fifth, the *throat* chakra (*vishuddha*), is located in front of the throat. The sixth is the *brow* chakra (*ajna*), located between the eyebrows, also known as the "*third-eye*". The seventh, the *crown* chakra (*sahasrara*), is located on the top of the head.

Each chakra has its own color and is divided into a different number of segments, resembling a wheel with its spokes, with the fewest in the root chakra and ascending in numbers toward the crown chakra. As a rule, it is bright and luminous.

As is the case with everything, almost, there are other versions of the chakra system that offer more or less than these main principal seven, starting from five through six and on to the famous seven ones, to eight, nine, or twelve and more. The number of segments differs, also, in different schools and approaches, reaching millions in some instances, so there is no definitive description about them on which to rely with confidence, but the chakras are a constant and important item in the toolbox of the Seeker, nevertheless.

Their importance originates from the fact that contemplating them and concentrating on them, as suggested before, strengthens and develops the various faculties present in our physical body, especially in the cerebral-spinal-glandular structure.

The chakras can be sorted in three groups. The first and the second are *physiological* chakras; they absorb the vital energy for our existence. The *personal* chakras—the third, fourth and the fifth, are connected to the astral and mental bodies. The *spiritual* chakras, the sixth and the seventh, are connected to the pituitary and pineal gland, respectively. On this relation, more in the "Head" section, after this.

These centers, being of an energetic nature, are activated by the forces of the universe and of the earth, as well as by the force of 'kundalini' that resides in us in the *root* chakra.

The chakras are active in everyone. They rotate in a certain rhythm, in synchronicity with each other, in clockwise direction. In each individual, the size of the chakras, their appearance and their operation are in direct proportion to his personal development in all aspects, physical, mental and spiritual, so in a person more developed, the chakras are bigger and rotate faster, while being more, or even fully synchronized; they are brighter and more luminous. In undeveloped persons, they are active in the most basic manner, which means that they are small, faded, rotate slowly and are unsynchronized, mostly.

The important issue in this regard, is the possibility to enhance or hasten the proper development of the chakras, or accomplish both, by deliberate actions on our part to this end. Several means are available for this task. Some are, or should be, done by us as a matter of routine while on the quest for the Divine, as explained in all of the previous sections of the book in many forms and places, while others, concentration and visualization specifically, should be employed deliberately. A short reminder of the routine means and an explanation of the concentration and visualization tools to this end, follows.

Proper *input* and *output* to our body and from it in all its aspects, and proficient actions on our part should be done routinely.

On the side of the input, we have to provide proper food for the physical body, while avoiding excesses in quantity and being mindful of its quality, according to what has been detailed in the section about the use of toxic substances.

Proper care of our body, keeping it clean, trim and fit, is another routine requirement. In this regard, it would be worth mentioning that in India, there are yogis who practice what would seem extreme and bizarre self-cleansing methods, to the average person. For example, cleaning the sinuses with a thread inserted in the nose in one nostril, then pushing it out of the nose through the other nostril and then pulling it back and forth for a few minutes, or cleansing the bowels, by pulling them out and cleaning them. To such extremes, there is no need to go maybe, but these examples serve to show the importance of a clean, trim and fit body that some pursue in any form.

Assimilation and integration of proper principles, those compatible with The Law of Universal Love, would be another means for proper *input*. The application of principles in accordance with the Law of Universal Love would be the *output* side of the effort. Entertainment of proper thoughts for the mental body—positive, non-judgmental and unattached, will lead to subtler and more refined and congenial feelings, which in turn will lead to thoughts that are more positive, placing us in a better, more developed spiritual spot.

Concentration and visualization can be employed, and quite effectively, any time we wish to do so. The best way to do it, though, would be during the meditation sessions, where we can allot time for this special activity, a matter of a few minutes, only. This is done by concentrating on the various chakras, each in its turn, sequentially, starting from the *root* chakra, and visualizing them in the form of a trumpet stemming from our body, protruding only a few inches from it, vibrant and lively, big, shining, rotating clockwise in synchronicity with each other. This is akin to the chakra concentration technique described before.

It is important to know that the self-development of the chakras is not something to be taken lightly, which seems to be the unfortunate practice of quite a few Seekers. For a spiritually undeveloped person, or for one who is doing this just for the sake of it, the deliberate self-development of the root and the sex chakras can present an immediate danger because of the great energies unleashed in a body that is impure physically and mentally. Such a premature self-development can bring much turmoil that can torment the individual greatly. Strong and strange physical sensations and thoughts that sometimes can be terribly violent, revolving mainly around sex, are aroused in persons who are unaccustomed to such kind of energy, while sexual affinities present before the newly experienced symptoms, would be strengthened and pronounced.

For an excellent review of the chakras system and everything related to the subject, I recommend highly the book "The Chakras", published by the Theosophical Society.

The Head

From a spiritual point of view, the head is of a significance that cannot be exaggerated. Without it, there is no possibility to advance spiritually. From the physical point of view, it is the command post for an otherwise inert lump of flesh and bones. This assertion may sound misplaced, being so obvious, but it is important to emphasize it for a reason that is pertinent to our subject. The physical and the spiritual are intertwined in us inextricably, though from our physical vantage point, immersed in matter, we are incapable of recognizing and appreciating this as factual knowledge. The two facets of existence complement each other and are mutually dependant for proper functioning. Their final interactive combination is perpetually conducive to an ever-evolving human toward a more accomplished spiritual part of his, being able, when fully developed, to attain infinitely more, to encompass infinitely more, in acts as in thoughts, in understanding and in doing. Being able to understand more, because his mind will be able to reach farther, wider and deeper, he will be able to do more. This development is certain to come in the future for the entire human race. In this certain and unavoidable future development, the head plays a decisive part. If this development is important to us, and I think it is, then, as in the passage about the possibility of self-development of the chakras, we can hasten this certain outcome by our own conscious actions, also. This is the aim of this section, to show how and with what we can do that, using our head for it.

The head was much revered in many cultures, and still is in certain primitive tribal communities, as the center of the individual's personality, as the epitome of one's entity and the place where the soul resides. It can be said with certainty that there was in practice, and still is, a *Cult of the Head*. Apparently, these people understood intuitively something that they could not know otherwise, or, a very remote possibility, it was something that was imparted to them from an outside source, still to be defined, and they retained it ritually as an acquired and sacred thing, not to be questioned.

As the place of the human personal essence—the soul, the head of a local hero was venerated as a protector of the locals and their surroundings, elevated to a degree of sanctity. Severed in battle from the corpse, or even from a living body, of an enemy, the head was kept, in various forms, as a relic, deemed to empower the keeper and his community over that enemy.

As a more factual example of the significance of the head, the following will be enlightening. In an archeological finding, an ancient skull was found in which there was a small and perfectly round cavity in its nape. This is known as skull trepanation, practiced widely since very ancient times, for which there can be two possible reasons. One would be a medical treatment for some ailment, maybe treating an internal hemorrhage, maybe to extract a wood or stone splint, or to remove broken pieces of fractured bones of the skull, but the small opening prohibits this possibility. Another, more convincing motive, could be ritual. It could be that the brain had been extracted, without destroying the skull, for preservation reasons, by way of sucking it through a small tube, maybe a reed, and then consuming it for the ritual reasons described above, that is, overcoming the enemy and empowering oneself with his essence. Then, after the procedure, the skull was preserved as a treasured trophy.

The main thing to know about the role that the head plays and, by far, the most important in regard to our spiritual development and the means to attain it, is that it is widely, and from very old times, perceived as the place where the *soul* resides. It is also perceived as the place where the wisdom that enables us to develop spiritually is received and assimilated.

The head is the place from which we can reach the Divine in us, the door to higher realms of existence, up to the highest. This is commonly accepted knowledge of the sages of all times in all cultures—that is, vertically—in time, and horizontally—in many cultures, thus adding much weight to its veracity by cross-verification as a means to ascertain authenticity of information. Sometimes, this knowledge is confused, contradictory or simply incoherent, but it all revolves around the same theme: If you want to **know**, if you want to **see**, if you want to "commune with the Divine", the head is the point from which to start, the place where the means for it can be found.

Ultimately, as mentioned throughout this book, anything and everything in us as well as in the world surrounding us, our thoughts as well as our acts, can be used as a means to achieve enlightenment, but, in the end, everything passes through the head, every experience, abstract and concrete. Together with many who think likewise, I am of the opinion, therefore, that the abilities existent in the head can be activated consciously toward the achievement of the ultimate goal, to find the Self and to reunite with it. All the other means used, internal—Kundalini Yoga, for example, or external—drugs, for example, which I do not condone in any way, end, literally and practically, in the head. "It's all in our head", as they say. And it is, indeed.

The crux of the matter is one or two glands that are to be found there. These are the *pineal* and the *pituitary* glands. The pineal is located in the center of the head, and the pituitary below it a little and about half way to the front of the head. To them, some add parts of the brain, in any combination—the *thalamus, the hypothalamus*, or the *corpus callosum*.

And why are they the crux of the matter? Well, because of a very important reason: the famous *Third Eye*.

A few words about this widely known term, the *third eye* are in order. From immemorial times, in the occult terminology, the term denotes a bodily organ of ours that enables us to "see beyond", that is, to perceive and comprehend things that reside in higher spheres than the one in which we live.

This ability consists of visions, clairvoyance and clairaudience, precognition and out-of-body-experience. This organ is said to reside in the head. Its location, there, is said to be behind the eyes, between the brows. But what, exactly, constitutes the third eye? Well, here the confusion begins.

Some say that the third eye is the *pineal* gland, others, that it is the *pituitary*. Others, still, that it is both of them together. To add to the confusion, some add to the mix the other parts of the brain mentioned above, the thalamus, the hypothalamus and the corpus callosum, all or in part.

And, for that matter, if the soul resides in the head, where is it located? The soul is treated to the same confusion, without having been allocated a definite place. The philosopher Descartes, mentioned by any and every book on spirituality as the source of this view, was of the opinion that the pineal gland is the place where the soul resides, but he was not the only one who stated this assertion. Since times immemorial, this was the accepted position on the subject and still is in the occult circles, before, around and after Descartes.

After all is said and for all we know, as far as objective knowledge can be attributed to occult information, the soul is very real, and the third eye exists as a very real organ, but the answer to the question where exactly these two integral parts of our being reside in us, is not definitive. The following is certain: the soul and the third eye inhabit the brain, but no one knows with certainty where.

The third eye resides in one of the mentioned glands – the pineal, the pituitary, or in both of them, or in any other configuration between them and the other parts of the brain mentioned. If the third eye resides in the same place with the soul or in a different place, is not known, either. My opinion on the matter is that a resident can inhabit only one place at a time, so the soul and the third eye can be only in one part of the brain, be it a gland or another part of it; and both may reside in the same place, sharing it, or each in a different single place. The possibility that they, each one or together, inhabit more than one part is quite illogical, because every part has its own, full and complex array of functions to perform. Therefore, if the third eye, and more so the soul, inhabit two or more parts, then this will hint that they are not an integer entity but a departmentalized one, which will be contrary to their nature.

Be it as it is, these two glands, the pineal and the pituitary, are of the utmost importance for our spiritual development. Their role, in this regard, is complementary to each other. The pituitary is attuned like a receiver to higher spheres of existence than the matter in which we reside, continuously receiving information from there in the form of cosmic principles of a supreme wisdom nature, as is to be expected of something originating from this source. The nature of this reception is akin, probably, to what is known as channeling, but performed unconsciously by us through this gland. This information is transferred to the pineal gland. In its turn, the pineal gland transforms these packets of data, which contain principles of spiritual knowledge and insights of a highly sophisticated nature, into principles that we, humans, can understand, assimilate, and then apply to our worldly existence.

From a spiritual point of view, this pair of glandular devices is one of the most important assets that we can have or aspire to. Without them, when trying to devise principles that will guide us on our way in this world, we would be left to our own devices, which originate in matter, and therefore are of a relative and transient nature instead of eternal and transcendental, able to refer to them only. Though not being conscious of it, having access to a supreme, eternal and transcendental, and so, indisputable source of knowledge, enables us to achieve the proper insight to a way of conduct that is compatible with the Law of Universal Love, the law that governs the Universe.

This hierarchical and interactive transfer of information of one kind and its transformation into another, is performed and accomplished with the help of physical means, those of hormonal secretions from each gland. Here, for their utmost importance, the *melatonin* and *serotonin* hormones, secreted by the pineal gland, are mentioned among others, but in particular the *melatonin* hormone.

As far as the spiritual development of the human race is concerned, though active physiologically, these very important glands, the pineal and the pituitary, are dormant now, so the occultists say, but a time will come when they will awake and fulfill their specific role in the unavoidable advance of humankind toward a fully accomplished spiritual facet. This role is to enable the human to connect and interact with higher realms of reality, fully aware of it.

The connection between the *glands* and the *chakras* presents another issue of confusion. The pituitary and the pineal glands are assigned to the sixth and to the seventh chakras, respectively, alternating between them in various schools.

Again, be it as it is, it is clear that in the occult, through all times and in all cultures that dealt with the subject, the glands in the head, of which, apparently, there was common knowledge, are considered most important in the human structure and spiritual attunement and development.

Prana

Prana means *life force* in Sanskrit, and, more specifically, it is equated with the *breath,* the *soul* and the *self.* It is an energy existent in all the forms of nature, from the littlest speck of dust to the most giant celestial bodies, organic and inorganic.

Its role cannot be overemphasized. It enables nature in all its forms, therefore us also, to make use of the various life's forces and sources, meaning energy in all its forms and the necessary material supplies—air, food, water and the sun's vitality and heat. It is the *spirit of the potential of life,* the Life Enabling Principle. It is not to be confounded with life itself.

Prana is absorbed by the body from its surroundings. We can increase the quantity absorbed in two ways: being aware of its presence and visualizing its entrance into our body, and breathing in a complete diaphragmatic manner. The best way to visualize its entrance into the body is through the crown chakra.

Prana can be used as a tool for our spiritual development in our quest for The Self, by channeling it to the specific parts of the body directly connected to it, the pineal and the pituitary glands.

The channeling is achieved by visualizing the prana making its way to these centers, infusing and filling them. This enhances our spiritual awareness, connectedness and powers, and with them, our healing powers, to ourselves and to others.

Benefits and Pitfalls of Spirituality and Meditation

That meditation has effects of various kinds, positive and negative, on the person engaging in this activity, is by now a foregone conclusion, attested by academic research since the very early '70s of the last century.

The subject caught the attention of the academic establishment when the Maharishi Mahesh Yogi, from India, brought his meditation technique, named Transcendental Meditation by him, to the West, following his predetermined plan to spread it universally. These researches, applied not only to TM, but to the meditation process in general, show a profoundly affecting influence on all the bodily functions. This influence originates in the state of relaxation induced by the process of meditation and in the improved ability to concentrate more intensely.

From physiological to physical performance, through mind and psyche state, all evidence showed improvement. Physiological functions such as metabolism, blood pressure, heart rate, respiration, showed reduction, and so, were improved. Brain functionality—memory, perception, intelligence growth, learning ability and more, showed improvement also. Hormonal secretion was enhanced; athletes did better in the arena; the ability to cope with different social and personal issues improved; the immune system was strengthened; the mortality rate in different old-age groups declined, or to put it in another way, life was prolonged.

Healing of hard illnesses and even regression of cancer, had also been observed, leading to the presentation of meditation as a remedial means instead of drugs. The relaxing influence of the meditation process in particular, is receiving, nowadays, special attention in the medical establishment across the health-care field, but more so, the influence that its beneficial influence in reducing stress has on the immune system, by fortifying it.

In short, it is as if a magic wand touches the body of the meditating person, improving and enhancing his state of being in every aspect, literally.

Of course, the individual constitution and initial state of health and being are to be considered, so all those benefits can be of much measure for one and of less for another.

On the other hand, though the predominant findings in these academic researches show that the meditation process has positive influence, other researches show that it has negative influences, also.

If practiced too intensely or not as instructed, or by a spiritually undeveloped or underdeveloped person, or by a mentally unstable individual, it can lead to episodes of physical stress, such as muscular tension, or to episodes of mental problems, such as agitation, disassociation and disorientation, depersonalization, anxiety, altered perceptions and manic episodes. Such incidents may last minutes and sometimes months. During the meditation process proper and during the period of time that the Seeker is engaged in the spiritual, and some time after that, it is possible to encounter strange and sudden experiences of most any kind. Sensations of intense heat in the body, or of a strong sense of being uprooted from own personal frame of life and reality, are not uncommon.

To insure that such problems will not occur, one has, first, to be of sound mental state upon entering the spiritual realm. This forewarning is imperative and cannot be emphasized enough, nor exaggerated. Such sound mental state is required in order to be able to assimilate such disturbing experiences and to be able to encounter uncertainty and doubt without wincing; also, it requires the ability to encounter strong emotions and to be flexible enough to adapt and to absorb the experience.

Second, one has to be sure that he possesses a good knowledge of what is to be experienced, so as to be able to understand and to accept the meditation practice. Such knowledge is easily gathered from books, lectures and personal acquaintance with persons who are already on the spiritual path and who had experienced meditation for a long time.

Third, it is highly advisable to be associated with a group of people of the same mind; it provides support and mutual understanding and an unequivocal approval of such activity as positive and healthy.

Last word

We have reached the end of this tome dedicated to spirituality and to its best tool, meditation.

Reaching this point, allow me to thank you, dear reader, for giving me the privilege to present to you a package of information and knowledge that is different in many ways than the conventional one.

It is my fervent hope that reading it proved to be helpful in walking The Way, either as a beginner, or as a seasoned Seeker. If, as a beginner, you intend to follow this wondrous path, I wish you much success and satisfaction; if you already tread it, I wish you good use of the new bits of knowledge, if there were such for you. In either case, I wish you a pleasant walk and a fruitful spiritual development.

www.ingramcontent.com/pod-product-compliance
Ingram Content Group UK Ltd.
Pitfield, Milton Keynes, MK11 3LW, UK
UKHW020133250726
13967UKWH00002B/617

9 781425 150945